FELIPE HERNÁNDEZ

BEYOND MODERNIST MASTERS:
CONTEMPORARY ARCHITECTURE
IN LATIN AMERICA

BIRKHÄUSER
BASEL · BOSTON · BERLIN

The research for this publication was in part made possible by
the RIBA Research Trust and the Liverpool School of Architecture
Sabbatical scheme; we would like to express our thanks for
this generous support.

Graphic design
Miriam Bussmann, Berlin

Editor
Ria Stein, Berlin

Cover
House in Ribeirão Preto, Brazil

Photographer
Nelson Kon, São Paulo

Lithography
Licht + Tiefe, Berlin

Printing
fgb. freiburger graphische betriebe, Freiburg

Library of Congress Control Number: 2009910224

Bibliographic information published by the German National Library:
The German National Library lists this publication in the
Deutsche Nationalbibliografie; detailed bibliographic data is available
on the Internet at http://dnb.d-nb.de.

© 2010 Birkhäuser Verlag AG
Basel · Boston · Berlin
P.O.Box 133, CH-4010 Basel, Switzerland
Part of Springer Science+Business Media
Printed on acid-free paper produced from chlorine-free pulp. TCF ∞
Printed in Germany

ISBN 978-3-7643-8769-3

www.birkhauser.ch

9 8 7 6 5 4 3 2 1

CONTENTS

1 INTRODUCTION

Latin American cities and buildings continue to figure prominently in the history of architecture. Indeed, attention to architectural production in that part of the world has increased during the first decade of the 21st century. It can be argued that contemporary architects from Latin America are receiving more international recognition than ever before. Established European and North American magazines such as *Architectural Review*, *Architectural Record, Domus* and, even, non-specialised popular monthly publications such as *Casabella* and *Wallpaper* have dedicated numerous pages and special editions to recently finished buildings in Latin America. Similarly, there has been a proliferation of monographs about the work of contemporary Latin American architects; indeed, this book forms part of such a body of literature. What is more, architects from Latin American countries have won virtually all major architectural awards in the world in the past ten years.[1] The list of achievements could continue if I were to mention conferences, lecture series and visiting professorships at prestigious universities around the world. However, I do not intend to highlight the achievements of architects from Latin America. Instead, I would like to draw attention to the way in which such a degree of renewed international attention disrupts the somewhat homogenous image suggested by the banner 'Latin American architecture'. That is because the focus of such renewed attention has been diverted to new areas of architectural production. Rather than concentrating only on buildings produced during the middle years of the 20th century, by a reduced group of talented and enthusiastic modernist architects, recent publications focus on a younger generation of architects whose work differs greatly from that of their modernist predecessors. Not only is variation found in the form of buildings but, more importantly, in the themes and aspirations of contemporary young architects who work in some of the largest cities in the world, in conditions of poverty – and immense wealth – as well as in situations of social and political instability. The buildings designed by architects in Latin America during the past 20 years continue

COMISIÓN ECONÓMICA PARA AMÉRICA LATINA Y EL CARIBE (CEPAL), SANTIAGO DE CHILE, CHILE, CRISTIÁN DE GROOTE, EMILIO DUHART AND ROBERTO GOYCOLEA. VIEW OF THE FRONT AND MAIN ENTRANCE TO THE COMPLEX.

to display great formal creativity, but the above-mentioned conditions of practice demand more political awareness. As a result, schemes have become less ambitious in scale and more specific in scope. However, the nature of their work and the conditions of practice in contemporary Latin American countries impede the construction of a homogenous continental identity; even the existence of national identities is challenged by the diversity of architectural practices that participate in the continuous re-shaping of cities in Latin America.

In spite of a resurgent interest, the bulk of literature in existence about architectures in Latin America, especially the material published in the English language, focuses on modern architecture. In fact, many recent books set a chronological limit between 1929 and 1960 as the most representative period of architectural production in the continent. Two of those books are Valerie Fraser's *Building the New World: Studies in the Modern Architecture of Latin America 1930–1960* and the volume entitled *Latin American Architecture 1929–1960: Contemporary Reflections* edited by Carlos Brillembourg. Other volumes published around the same time are Malcolm

COMISIÓN ECONÓMICA PARA AMÉRICA LATINA Y EL CARIBE (CEPAL). COVERED CIRCULATION.

Quantrill's *Latin American Architecture: Six Voices*, a book in which six critics examine the work of six modernist architects from six Latin American countries, and Elisabetta Andreoli's and Adrian Forty's *Brazil's Modern Architecture*, a book which expresses, in the first sentence, how reliant Latin American architectures are on the work of only a few modernist architects – those I will refer to, in this book, as the modernist masters.[2] Amongst the most influential modernist masters are Luis Barragán, Paulo Mendes da Rocha, Oscar Niemeyer, Rogelio Salmona and Carlos Raúl Villanueva. There are, however, numerous other figures who played an important role in the dissemination of architectural modernism throughout the continent, for example: Eladio Dieste (Uruguay), Cristiàn de Groote (Chile), Gorka Dorronsoro (Venezuela), Carlos Mijares (Mexico) and Clorindo Testa (Argentina), to mention only a few. Although the work of this latter group of architects has not received the same amount of international exposure, their buildings contributed greatly to the development of architectural ideas in their countries and the construction, by international scholars, of a homogenous continental identity based on modern architecture.

Undoubtedly, the period between 1929 and 1960 was one of great change for most nations in the continent. It was a period of transition when primarily agrarian economies transformed irregularly into a state of industrialisation. By irregular transformation, I refer to the fact that industrialisation did not happen simultaneously in all nations across the continent and that, even at the interior of each country, it was not a smooth process. Industrialisation brought along a new economic system which resulted in greater socio-economic disparity and political instability. There was, for example, great tension between different forms of nationalism: those who promulgated the recuperation of past traditions – pre-Columbian or indigenous and, even, colonial customs – and those which subscribed to modernist principles of progress and universalisation. Socialist ideas thrived. There were also dissident political groups and, at the other end of the spectrum, many right-wing regimes in various countries throughout the continent. Multiple factors influenced the socio-political instability which characterised this historical period. Yet, they all were related, in one way or another, to the enormous transformations caused by the decline of the prevailing feudal-agrarian system and the emergence of a precarious

COMISIÓN ECONÓMICA PARA AMÉRICA LATINA Y EL CARIBE (CEPAL). COURTYARD.

industrialisation, what I refer to with the expression 'a state of industrialisation'. This is because industrialisation did not result in the consolidation of 'industrialised societies', or economies, but in a broad range of 'versions of industrialisation' which suited the interests of national elites. In other words, local elites wanted to retain the privileges that the previous system granted them, while taking advantage of the benefits brought about by industrial development.

Comprehensibly, liberal governments in many Latin American nation-states embraced modern architecture during this unstable period because it suited the rhetoric of progress that they promulgated. At a time when cities were growing rapidly due to the increasing migration of people from the countryside to the main cities, modern architecture seemed capable of providing the necessary solutions to guarantee good standards of life for everyone, while also stimulating economic development. Since the technology to produce modern architecture was not entirely available in every country, its very implementation motivated industrial development by instigating the creation of factories to produce cement, steel and glass, materials that are necessary for the construction of modern buildings. It was the

image of modernity – cultural dynamism, industrialisation and economic expansion   which persuaded politicians to endorse modern architecture enthusiastically.

NATION-BUILDING AND UNIVERSALISATION: THE ERA OF LARGE-SCALE BUILDING

The post-war period (1945–1960) was a time when most Latin American economies flourished. Economic buoyancy allowed governments to build on a large scale that was unconceivable in other parts of the world; especially in Europe, where most countries endured a period of austerity. Moreover, architects in Latin America were given *carte blanche* to pursue their aesthetic, technical, functional and urban aspirations in order to materialise their idealistic plans for buildings and cities. Suddenly, Latin America became an attractive destination for European and North American architects who saw an opportunity to materialise their own projects there – the figure of Le Corbusier stands out unrivalled amongst the architects who came to find work in Latin America at the time. Grand and optimistic programmes designed to instigate development gave an opportunity to local

IGLESIA DE CRISTO OBRERO, ATLÁNTIDA, URUGUAY, ELADIO DIESTE. VIEW OF THE UNDULATING CORNICE ALONG THE SIDEWALLS.

IGLESIA DE CRISTO OBRERO. VIEW OF THE SPIRAL STAIRCASE.

and European architects alike to undertake the construction of governmental buildings, university campuses, mass housing, airports, museums, stadia and even entire cities.

One of the most remarkable examples of large-scale modern architecture in this period is the Universidad Nacional Autónoma de México (UNAM), built between 1947 and 1952. The master plan corresponds with the principles of CIAM urbanism, although it also incorporates pre-Columbian strategies of land occupation, such as terracing and the construction of pedestals to magnify the image of significant buildings – a strategy that resembles the organisation of Aztec settlements. Similarly, most buildings of the plan subscribe to the five points of architecture formulated by Le Corbusier in 1926, although some incorporate contrasting elements, i. e. decorative motifs taken from the local indigenous tradition. A building which juxtaposes different elements is the Central Library designed by Juan O'Gorman in collaboration with Gustavo Saavedra and Juan Martínez de Velasco. Generally speaking, the library is a conventional concrete slab construction which rests on a plinth. Large expanses of glass around the plinth reveal the floating planes and the free-standing concrete columns in the interior. Above the plinth rests the tower, a large rectangular volume whose exterior is decorated with colourful images of *mestizo* workers and soldiers, Aztec symbols and other pagan motifs. Such a juxtaposition exposes contrasting interpretations of the nation's cultural identity, an inherent ambivalence in the construction of Mexico by the popular imagination. On the one hand, the planners of the university campus and the architects of the library identified themselves with modern architecture,

as seen in the use of a particular formal repertoire, certain construction techniques and, even, the methods of design used (plans, sections, elevations and perspective views). On the other hand, there is a distinct reluctance to abandon their pre-Columbian past where they continue to find many traits of their identity. In other words, this shows that Mexican architects were split between ideas of progress, industrialisation and technological advancement while, simultaneously, holding a desire for the recuperation of an indigenous past they felt proud of. Far from negative, these inherent contradictions reflect the particularities of Mexican politics and culture at the time. It is precisely these contradictions which assign great architectural merit to the campus and its buildings: instead of offering a deceiving sense of homogeneity, the university campus emerges as a true representation of the Mexican identity – heterogeneous, unequal and ambivalent.

Another example of the large-scale projects built during this period is the Ciudad Universitaria de Caracas, designed by Carlos Raúl Villanueva between 1944 and 1970. Without doubt, this was Villanueva's most significant project, not only because of the vast scale and the time he invested in its design and construction but, also, because it shows multiple aspects of his expression as an architect. The master plan, for example, subscribes to the principles of modern urbanism while the buildings show a progression of various styles. From the symmetrical and heavy Hospital Clínico on the east, to the lighter and more fluid forms of the recreational zone on the west (which comprises the Olympic stadium, the swimming pool and the baseball stadium) passing through the cultural and administrative zone at the heart of campus, which contains the famous covered plaza and the Aula Magna. Since Venezuela did not have as rich a pre-Columbian heritage as Mexico, the implementation of modern architecture did not meet heavy opposition from nationalist groups whose members wanted to evoke an indigenous past.[3] Instead, the oil economy which transformed a poor agrarian country into a prosperous nation-state, brought with it a new sense of historical optimism. Rather than indigenous and revolutionary motifs, as in the Mexican university campus examined above, Villanueva associated himself with North American ideas and the European avant-garde in order further to emphasise the image of national prosperity.

Needless to say, the largest and most significant project realised during this period was Brasilia. Paradoxically, it was inaugurated in 1960, as if closing the era of modern architecture in Latin America. Indeed, as Valerie Fraser points out, Brasilia was 'one ambition too far, and the architectural establishment in the USA and Europe turned against it'.[4] After studying the plans for Brasilia in his 1958 graduate seminar at Harvard, Sigfried Giedion and his students concluded that they were inadequate. In their opinion, the Brazilian government should have appointed international planning experts or, even, commissioned Le Corbusier to assist. Clearly the Euro-American establishment considered Brazilian architects capable of designing good buildings, but an entire city was beyond their capability; the Brazilians were not prepared to design their own capital city – a project which could only be accomplished successfully with the assistance of the experts from Europe or North America. Giedion's damning declaration was supported by other critics and historians – as I will demonstrate below – and, so, interest in modernist Latin American production decreased rapidly.

Despite derogatory statements such as Giedion's, Brasilia remains a remarkable example of modern architecture worthy of examination. Its political backers and the architects conceived Brasilia as a sign of progress and economic expansion, as well as the symbol of a culturally vibrant and confident nation. These ideas were to materialise in three ways: the realisation of the plan itself with its urban and public infrastructure, the construction of emblematic buildings (i.e. the capitol building, the palace of congress, the ministries, the cathedral and so on) and through the provision of mass housing (an aspect included in the later stages of development). Of the three aspects, housing is the only one that has direct impact on the common people – the other two do not affect directly the lives of the majority of the population. However, it is precisely this aspect, housing, which reveals the detachment between the elites – amongst whom architects are included – and the common people. A brief

NATIONAL CONGRESS, BRASILIA, BRAZIL, OSCAR NIEMEYER.

look at the objectives for the provision of housing in Brasilia is enough to reveal this severance. In a periodical called *Brasilia*, published by the corporation in charge of planning, building and administering the city, the expectations set on the provision of mass housing were described thus:

'As for the apartments themselves, some are larger and some are smaller in the number of rooms. [They] are distributed, respectively, to families on the basis of the number of dependants they have. And because of this distribution, the residents of a *superquadra* are forced to live as if in the sphere of one big family, in perfect social coexistence, which results in benefits for the children who live, grow up and study in the same environment of sincere camaraderie, friendship and wholesome upbringing. [...] And thus [are] raised, on the plateau, the children who will construct the Brazil of tomorrow, since Brasilia is the glorious cradle of a new civilization.'[5]

The US-American anthropologist James Holston, who wrote one of the harshest critiques that exists of Brasilia, shows the way in which people were inscribed in the narratives of progress and nationalism as a homogenous community. Indeed, in the process of imagining a homogenous national community, peoples are removed from their historical pasts – the use of plural is not only appropriate but necessary – in order to conceive the idea of 'perfect social coexistence'. The carefully crafted statement cited above discloses the desire of Brazilian politicians to be part of modernity, not simply as an architectural construction but as a western discourse of civilisation. The architects, on the other hand, were understandably busy trying to realise an exemplary city with which to demonstrate that they

NATIONAL CONGRESS.

INTERSECTION OVER THE *RODOVIÁRIA*, BRASILIA'S BUS TERMINAL,
CONGESTED AND OCCUPIED BY PEOPLE.

were capable of producing architecture of the same quality as their European and North American counterparts and, even, better than theirs. So, Brasilia was thought to be the origin of a renewed thoroughly modern nation, but, in the process, it disowned the heterogeneous realities and convoluted histories of the nation's peoples.

Paradoxically, like Giedion's, most critiques of Brasilia – including Holston's – focus largely on the physical dimension of the city: its form, its buildings, the fact that it seems always to be empty and so on. People, the city's inhabitants, only figure negatively as antagonistic elements that prevent the full realisation of the architects' plans. Holston, for example, points out that various parts of the city have been altered by people in the course of its 50 years of existence, alterations which are considered to be detrimental to the original plan. For Holston, the fact that people have transformed physically parts of the city in order to carry out their daily activities, or in order to introduce unplanned uses which subvert the original zoning arrangement, is a testimony of the failure of the city. He refers mainly to the *rodoviária* (Brasilia's bus terminal), one of the most populated parts of the city today.[6]

Consultants to other organisations such as UNESCO seem to share Holston's point of view. The statement for the inclusion of Brasilia in the list of World Heritage sites underlines that:

'Brasilia currently has a privileged population of 300,000 people, and a large, often transitory, population distributed among the seven satellite cites, as well as in the poorer neighbourhoods that were established to the *detriment* of the 1956–1957 project. In the absence of both a master plan and a code of urbanism, the standards defined by Costa and Niemeyer have been *infringed* upon in the greatest *disarray* [my emphasis].'[7]

By declaring the actions and physical transformations carried out by the city's inhabitants 'detrimental', UNESCO denies political agency to the people in the construction of their own inhabitable space. Paradoxically, the severance of architecture from the realm of the social contradicts the very notion of heritage as a cultural representation of a people's history. UNESCO's assessment implies that there is a need to reconnect the city, in its current status of inhabitation, with its 'original' empty and idealised version which is found in the drawings produced by Lucio Costa, and the buildings designed by Oscar Niemeyer, more than half a century ago. The question arises, for whom is Brasilia a heritage, for its own inhabitants or for an international (and largely anonymous) community of architectural conservationists?

The arguments put forward in this book contest such a derogatory inscription of people in the continued construction of cities, and in the re-signification of buildings. Rather than having a negative effect, the emergence of satellite cities – or spontaneous settlements and shanty towns – and the appropriations carried out by the residents of Brasilia are a testimony of the city's success. It is precisely through their acts of appropriation that residents introduce their own and varied socio-cultural traditions into a city that was openly designed to restrain heterogeneity. As a result, the inhabitants of Brasilia are considered to be the producers of social, cultural and physical spaces that represent the tense interaction between different groups and the conflictive socio-political realities of Brasilia and the rest of the country. If there is a reason why Brasilia has been successful, it is not only because of the compliance of its master plan with the principles of modern urbanism expressed in the CIAM manifestos or in the Athens Charter, nor is it because of the elegance of its modernist buildings. The success of Brasilia lies also in the fact that it has demonstrated the un-realisability of homogenising nationalist discourses – according to which people can live in 'perfect social coexistence' – and the impossibility to contain the people in the horizontal space of an 'imagined community', to borrow Benedict Anderson's powerful term.[8] Brasilia makes visible the heterogeneity and dynamism of Brazilian cultures and societies, their historical discontinuities and the way in which their struggle for survival and identification materialises itself in the transformation of the city and its surroundings. In other words, Brasilia is a successful city, and represents a heritage both for its own inhabitants and the world alike, simply because it turned out to be like any other city.

Many of the case studies examined in this book show that contemporary architects have developed alternative strategies to deal with the existence of cultural difference and the effects that such difference has on the fabric of cities and buildings. Contemporary architects decidedly disagree with the narratives of modernity, i. e. (linear) progress and universalisation. Instead, they embrace socio-cultural heterogeneity both enthusiastically and critically, and see the constantly shifting political and economic circumstances in which Latin American people live as sources of inspiration to carry out typological innovations. That is why, in recent years, there has been a noticeable change in the scale of the projects promoted by national and local govern-

ments, as well as in the aspirations of contemporary young architects. Plans for entire cities and punctual mega-projects are rare nowadays. Instead, attention is given to specific issues in precise areas of cities. More importantly, geographical, social and political specificity also allow architects more accurately to attend the needs of particular social groups so that buildings are more closely connected with people.

THE INSCRIPTION OF LATIN AMERICAN BUILDINGS IN THE HISTORY OF MODERN ARCHITECTURE

I have brought forward these three examples of architectural modernism in the period between 1929 and 1960 – the campus of the Universidad Nacional Autónoma de México in the Mexican capital, the campus of the Universidad Central de Venezuela in Caracas and Brasilia – not because they are the only examples to be found in Latin America, nor is it my intention to imply that they have greater historical or socio-political significance than others. In fact there are numerous instances of extraordinary modern architecture throughout the continent; so many indeed that a great deal always remains inevitably unmentioned. Drawing attention to the critiques of modern Latin American buildings, or to stress the apparent dissociation between architecture and people, is by no means an attempt to take away architectural merit from any of them. The three cases mentioned above, and the many others which have been omitted for reasons of space, are unquestionably great buildings in their own right and examples of the way in which architects

PEDREGULHO HOUSING COMPLEX, RIO DE JANEIRO, BRAZIL, AFFONSO EDUARDO REIDY.

UNIVERSIDAD CENTRAL DE VENEZUELA, CARACAS, VENEZUELA, CARLOS RAÚL VILLANUEVA. VIEW OF THE COVERED PLAZA.

UNIVERSIDAD CENTRAL DE VENEZUELA. FOYER OF THE AULA MAGNA.

from Latin America appropriated modern architecture in their countries. These buildings caught the attention of international commentators at the time and, so, Latin America was inscribed in the history of architecture. Their inscription, however, was not an innocuous act. Latin American architectures were – in fact, continue to be – inscribed in the history of the field according to European and North American norms. Its inscription had to be sanctioned by European and North American critics or historians. Let me give a few examples before discussing the implications of this mode of historical inscription.

Referring to the Pedregulho Housing Complex (1950–1952) in Rio de Janeiro, a social housing scheme designed by Affonso Eduardo Reidy, Valerie Fraser points out that 'in the 1954 "Report on Brazil" [published] in the *Architectural Review* it was the one project singled out by Walter Gropius, Max Bill and Ernesto Rogers for unqualified praise. Bill described it "as completely successful from the standpoint of town planning as it is architecturally and socially":'[9] In fact, as Fraser indicates, architects and critics from around the world, mainly from the USA, visited Brazil – and other countries in South and Central America – on a regular basis in order to observe how local practitioners were appropriating modern architecture. Visitors, then, passed judgement about the quality of the work produced by local architects and determined whether their buildings accomplished successfully the standards set by the European and North American architectural establishment. Of course, approval granted inclusion in the history of architecture, while disapproval led to their exclusion and, ultimately, to their historical inexistence.

For another example let us return to Carlos Raúl Villanueva who, unlike Brazilian architects, did not receive international

recognition during the period in question (1929–1960). Only in the past 20 years has his work been fully presented to an international audience, a process in which his daughter Paulina Villanueva, also an architect, has played an important role: she published a monograph about the work of her father in the year 2000.[10] Interestingly, in the book's preface, the publisher and editor, Raúl Rispa, feels compelled to establish the credentials of C. R. Villanueva by indicating that his work has been mentioned in books written by renowned figures such as Leonardo Benevolo, William Curtis, Kenneth Frampton and Nikolaus Pevsner. In other words, the architectural value of the work of C. R. Villanueva is not found in its intrinsic characteristics, nor does it lie in the way it responds to specific circumstances or resolves the needs of the people to whom it was addressed, but in the fact that European critics have considered it to be worthy. In the rest of the book, P. Villanueva describes her father's buildings by way of comparison with European and North American referents, comparisons which establish similarity rather than difference. Thus, it transpires that the architectural achievement of C. R. Villanueva lies in his ability successfully to employ the formal repertoire of modern architecture – which confirms the view of the editor.

A final example is Alejandro Aravena, principal of ELEMENTAL, Chile, who has recently established his own credentials and those of his practice by listing all the prizes that they have been awarded – as most architects do in a fiercely competitive profession – and, also, by highlighting the fact that their work has been included in the latest edition of Kenneth Frampton's *Modern Architecture: A Critical History*. Such an apparently insignificant addition to the promotional material of the practice (available on their website), reveals the persistent significance

UNIVERSIDAD CENTRAL DE VENEZUELA. RAMP LEADING TO THE AULA MAGNA.

HOSPITAL CLÍNICO, UNIVERSIDAD CENTRAL DE VENEZUELA.

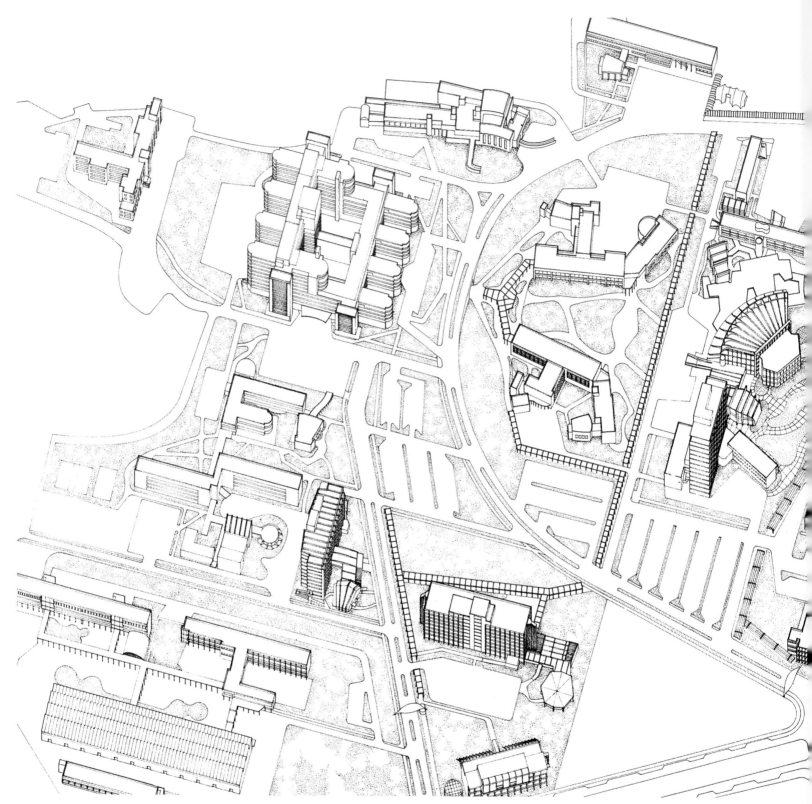

UNIVERSIDAD CENTRAL DE VENEZUELA. AXONOMETRIC VIEW OF THE MASTER PLAN.

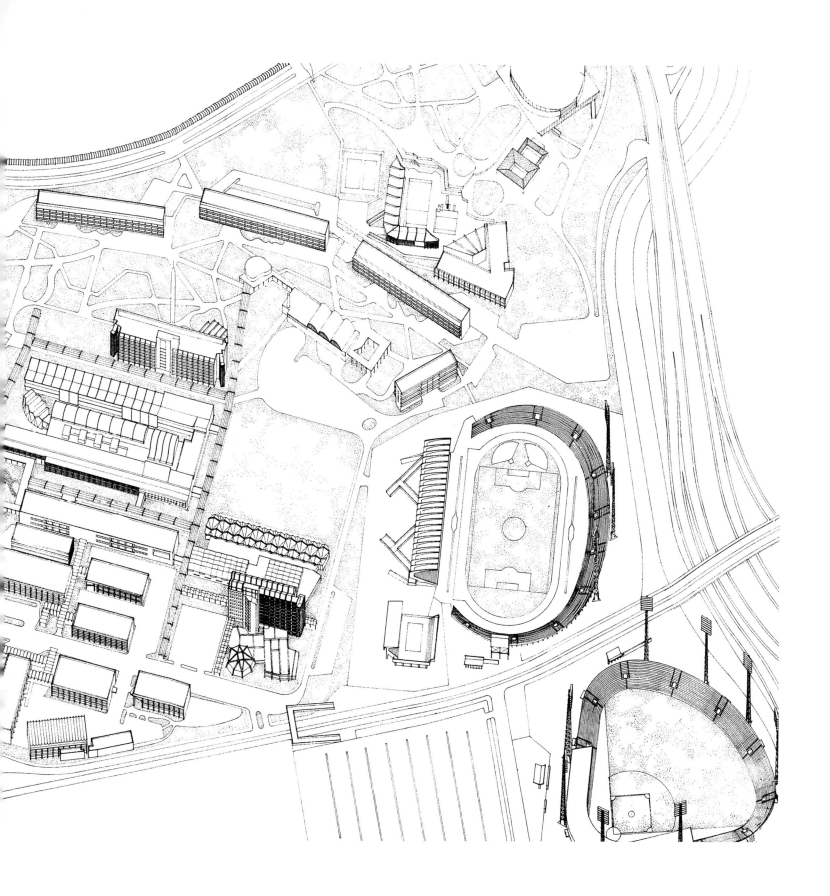

of obtaining the approval of the Euro-American architectural apparatus. Indeed, it is only through inclusion in the distinctly singular history of architecture which continues to be written mainly by European and North American scholars, that buildings produced in Latin America (and the non-west, or South, or Orient, depending on what scholarly stream one subscribes to) appear to have any architectural value. These attitudes indicate that a hierarchical structure still exists in the world of architecture, a structure which places European and North American architectural narratives in a dominant position. While it is somewhat understandable that Euro-American architects and historians construct a system of architectural critique which permits them to preserve their authority over non-western practices, it is somewhat alarming that Latin American architects appear voluntarily to subscribe to it. On the other hand, their deliberate compliance with such a system of referentiality could be seen as an act of resistance, as I will discuss later.

The straightforward comparison of buildings produced in Latin American countries with European and North American referents does not mean that modernist architects in the former territory did not have any creativity or that they were merely subservient copy-cats. As Fraser remarks, 'Latin American modern architecture [...] is not an uncritical reworking of European modernism with the addition of some decorative local colour, but a deliberate and more profound adaptation of or challenge to European models'.[11] However, unlike Fraser, who seems to welcome the 'adaptations of and challenges to' European modernism, there are critics who react negatively. William Curtis, for example, in his seminal book *Modern Architecture since 1900*, refers to Latin American architecture in unmistakably derogatory terms.[12] In the first paragraph of the 27th chapter of his book, entitled 'The Process of Absorption: Latin America, Australia and Japan' Curtis affirms that the modern movement in architecture was 'the intellectual property of certain countries in Western Europe, of the United States and of some parts of the Soviet Union'. With the use of legal terminology, Curtis unequivocally assigns the rights of authorship to a select group of western countries, which in his eyes are the only possessors of modern architectural knowledge. Such categorical affirmation is followed by another stunning pronouncement: in Curtis' opinion, 'by the end of the 1950s, *transformations*, *deviations* and *devaluations* [my emphasis] of modern architecture had found their way to many other areas of the world'.[13] With this statement Curtis dismisses categorically modern architectural production in Latin America, Australia and Japan during the 1940s and 1950s. Throughout the entire chapter, Curtis is at pains to stress the fact that developing countries *received* modern architecture

from Europe mainly via the work of Le Corbusier. It is clear that for Curtis the dissemination of modern architecture follows a genealogy which finds its roots in Europe and develops via the work of an exclusive selection of architects (mainly European). It is somewhat amusing how Curtis emphasises the links between Latin American architectures and some form of a European predecessor. For example his description of the university campus in Mexico City reduces the project to 'a *competent* [my emphasis] version of Le Corbusier's Ville Radieuse, adjusted to the institutions and technology of Mexico'.[14] No further elaboration is necessary to understand which is the original, who was its author and who are the producers of what can only be called a competent version – transformation, deviation or devaluation – of the original.

As if that were not enough, later in the book (chapter 31, entitled 'Modernity, Tradition and Identity in the Developing World') Curtis continues his belittling account of non-western architectures. In his words, 'it was not until the 1940s and 1950s that modern forms had any appreciable impact on the "less developed" countries, and these forms were usually *lacking in the poetry and depth of meaning* [my emphasis] of the masterworks of the modern movement'.[15] This time Curtis accuses non-western architects of lacking in sensitivity and calls into question their architectural competence. Hardly could one find greater disparity in the historical inscription of Latin American modernism than in the statements presented by William Curtis and Max Bill (as quoted by Fraser above). Then again, that is precisely the ambivalence characteristic of such a mode of historical inscription. In fact, Curtis' own discourse is inhabited by contradiction. Towards the end of the book (chapter 34) he adopts a less unforgiving terminology in order to admit that some of the architectural explorations carried out by architects in the developing world – he refers here, specifically, to Mexico, Japan, Brazil, Palestine and South Africa – were 'judicious adjustments of generic features of modernism to the climates, cultures, memories and aspirations of their respective societies'.[16] Here, Curtis tries to reconcile the hierarchical bi-polar antagonism he had posited earlier in his book, yet it is clear that non-western architectures can only be presented in relation to the European and North American predecessor – and 'adjustment' of modernism.

Although Curtis does, indeed, inscribe Latin American architectural production in the history of modern architecture (in other words, buildings designed by architects in Latin America are documented historically), his methodological approach establishes a hierarchical system that places such production in a position of inferiority vis-à-vis the architectures of those countries of which modernism is the 'intellectual property'. This is achieved largely through strategies of disavowal which deny validity to the Other (Latin American modern architecture). Of course, this denial can only operate in relation to an assumed referential, hence superior, system: the European rational system which, in this case, is exemplified by the modern architectural discourse. That is why the non-western Other can only emerge in relation to European norms. However, the ambivalence detected in Curtis' method of historical inscription undermines the authority of his judgement. It is not that the authority of western architectural discourse is undermined – or that hierarchies are practically reversed – but that the claim for authority becomes questionable, open to scrutiny by the subjects of the derogation.

Let me now return to the idea of resistance. Referring to the promotional material produced by the firm ELEMENTAL in Chile, I questioned the fact that they use their inclusion in the latest edition of Kenneth Frampton's *Modern Architecture: A Critical History* as a means to establish their architectural credentials. It would seem rather contradictory to do so, when, as demonstrated above, non-western architectures always emerge in relation to dominant western norms and, so, never reach the same level of the predecessor. However, after examining the work of ELEMENTAL – as well as the work of other practices throughout the continent (see chapter 4 Designing for Poverty) – it appears that architects are embracing the very terms used to denigrate and affirm their inferiority as a counterpoint to the discourses that uphold the architectural superiority of Europe and North America. Rather than attempting to reproduce architectural models from the centres, many architects from Latin America deliberately produce 'transformations, deviations and devaluations' of the canon – to use Curtis' own derogatory terminology – in order to respond to the circumstances of change and instability in which poor Latin American people live. In their social housing schemes, architects like Aravena provide opportunities for people to complete – that is, to re-design, appropriate or customise – their dwellings and the public spaces that surround them. In so doing, the architect assigns agency to people as the producers of their own inhabitable space. In that sense, the negative aspects that, according to Holston and UNESCO, impede the realisation of cities (such a Brasilia), is turned into a creative mechanism that guarantees people's welfare and comfort while simultaneously increasing their sense of belonging. What is more, since buildings are always changing, it is no longer possible to judge the quality of architectural production on the basis of a referential system of universal applicability which focuses only on the form of buildings – nor

on a genealogy that traces the origin of architectural form back to Europe. Consequently, in embracing the terms used to discriminate their work and render it inferior, Latin American architects also unveil the inadequacy of existing methods of historical inscription.

CONTEMPORARY ARCHITECTURES IN LATIN AMERICA

The referential system that underpins the above-mentioned method of architectural historicisiation has permitted the construction of a coherent, linear and homogenous history which does not correspond with the realities of architectural production in most parts of the world, including the west. In the case of Latin America, for example, it has contributed to the creation of a deceitful image of architectural homogeneity projected through an exclusive selection of modernist buildings. As mentioned before, the work of architects like Luis Barragán, Oscar Niemeyer, Rogelio Salmona and Carlos Raúl Villanueva, amongst others, has been praised by international commentators primarily because it reaches a high degree of refinement in relation to their Euro-American counterparts – whose work sets the standard. Rather than attempting to present 'Latin American architecture' as a homogenous body made of buildings which comply with hegemonic Euro-American narratives, this book demonstrates that there is great heterogeneity in the work of contemporary architects throughout the continent. Diversity and difference are not only visible between countries but, also, within countries. Moreover, given the great socio-political disparity that exists in Latin American societies, architects often need to employ a variety of design methods and, so, never develop a personal style – in fact, a younger generation of contemporary architects refuses actively to do so. Indeed, this is a trait that sets the current generation of architects apart from the modernist masters, who expressed their individual identities through very personal formal repertoires and material palettes.

Contemporary architects also need to adapt themselves to new forms of practice increasingly determined by contract laws, social responsibility, insurance liabilities and tremendous monetary fluctuations. Hence, the figure of the sole practitioner is rapidly being replaced by associations and, often, temporary consortia which allow architects to transcend national boundaries and operate internationally. Again, this is another aspect covered in this book which differs greatly from the way in which the masters of modernism conducted their practices. Though there were a few exceptions, modernist architects – those whose practices flourished between 1929 and 1960 – built only in their own countries. Many were trained abroad and worked

LAS TORRES DEL PARQUE, BOGOTÁ, COLOMBIA, ROGELIO SALMONA.

masters. The practice of comparing buildings produced in the region with 'precedents' from other parts of the world has been avoided for two reasons. First, it allows to circumvent the hegemonic system of referentiality inherent in such a form of historical analysis; since anteriority grants authority on grounds of originality, comparative analyses inevitably (re)construct, or reinforce, hegemonic architectural systems of judgement. Second, it requires the critic to focus on issues different from form and, so, to bring forward the historical, socio-cultural and political dimensions of architecture in each particular case. This kind of analysis does not imply that form is not important; formal concerns are inseparable from architecture. Indeed, the form of each building in this book is described in traditional and simple terms. However, emphasis is given to issues regarding people, their history, culture and the social, political and economic circumstances in which they live. In other words, each case study is considered as a site-specific exercise and, so, its form is examined in relation to its own context, context understood in the broadest sense of the term, not merely as a set of physical and environmental factors. I am by no means implying that there is no connection between Latin American and architectures in other parts of the world, nor am I trying to suggest that European and North American narratives no longer influence the work of architects in Latin America. Far from that, contemporary Latin American architects are more intricately connected with the rest of the world than ever before, as I indicated at the beginning of this introduction. Hence, the purpose of the proposed style of analysis is not to allege cultural autonomy but to reinforce the link between buildings produced in Latin America and the people who use them.

The book is organised in five chapters. The first, 'Building on the City's Edge', examines six buildings located on the peripheries or on the edges between planned and unplanned areas of cities. The accelerated expansion of Latin American cities since the middle of the 20th century proved that urban planning strategies were inadequate to deal with rapid change and, also, with the ingenuity brought to bear by common people in the construction of neighbourhoods and entire parts of cites. For years, governments tried to eliminate spontaneous settlements, usually by relocating poor people to the outskirts. As the vast majority of relocation programmes failed, new strategies have been developed in order to improve the living conditions of people in poor areas without resorting to traumatic, and often violent, mass relocation programmes. A method that has proven successful is the punctual insertion of educational, recreational and communal facilities. Instead of rendering the poor invisible by relocating them outside cities, current programmes increase

for other architects such as Le Corbusier, Walter Gropius, Bruno Zevi and Louis I. Kahn, to mention a few, prior to setting their own offices. However, once they were established as individual practitioners their work was largely limited to their own countries. Today, on the other hand, architects build regularly in neighbouring countries and also in other continents.

In order to dismantle the deceitful sense of homogeneity conveyed by studies which focus only on projects of the modernist period, this book examines different types of buildings, in different cities and geographical locations. The case studies examined in this book have been designed by an assortment of established architects as well as by young practitioners. The book illustrates exciting formal experiments and the use of new technologies, as well as more serene buildings made of traditional materials, many of which are built by local craftsmen with scarce resources. In all, this book encompasses a wider range of themes and design methods which highlight the architectural heterogeneity that exists in Latin America today.

Each case study in this book is analysed in its own milieu. Comparisons with other buildings are deliberately not drawn unless it is necessary to point out internal differences in the work of individual architects or variation in relation to the modernist

FONDO DE CULTURA ECONÓMICA (GABRIEL GARCÍA MÁRQUEZ CULTURAL CENTRE), BOGOTÁ, COLOMBIA, ROGELIO SALMONA. VIEW OF THE SUCCESSION OF COURTYARDS AND CIRCULATIONS AT VARIOUS LEVELS.

FONDO DE CULTURA ECONÓMICA. MAIN ACCESS SHOWING THE INTRICATE SOLUTION OF LEVELS AND CIRCULATIONS.

their visibility via the insertion of public facilities which, by contrast, often become conspicuous landmarks. These buildings bring benefits to poor areas and encourage the development of local communities at more manageable scales.

Similarly, the next chapter, 'Public Spaces as Contact Zones', looks at the way in which planned and unplanned areas of cities, as well as abandoned zones in the peripheries, are re-qualified as zones of socio-cultural encounter and interaction. The term 'contact zone', as used by Mary Louise Pratt, refers to areas where different groups of people meet and intermingle.[17] It has to be emphasised that contact zones are not areas where differences are resolved and harmonious consensus is reached. On the contrary, contact zones are sites of irresolution where cultural differences are acted out, made visible, negotiated on a continuous basis, although not necessarily resolved. The term is appropriate for the study of projects whose aim is to patch up, as it were, different parts of cities which had become fragmented, or abandoned, for historical reasons. Architects in this chapter have taken the challenge of designing public spaces which allow for multiple activities to take place, permanent and itinerary, and which encourage appropriation by the public. Despite such tasks, architects do not relinquish their interest

in form, or formal exploration. On the contrary, the projects included in the first and second chapters of this book show that architects can articulate successfully their own personal agendas with the encouragement of community participation.

The following chapter, 'Designing for Poverty', tackles a theme that is regularly excluded from books on Latin American architecture: social housing. For a number of reasons, many of which are related to the incredibly tight budgets allocated to social housing, architectures for the poor never receive sufficient scholarly attention.[18] The study of social housing is undertaken in one of three ways: it is totally excluded from architecture books; it is reduced to a few back pages and footnotes; or it is addressed in separate publications which are, more often than not, written by professionals in other fields such as sociology, anthropology, urban geography. Only when projects correspond with particular international trends, as in the case of Eduardo Affonso Reidy and Carlos Raúl Villanueva, do social housing schemes attain centrefold status. However, this book brings to the fore the efforts made, and innovative solutions produced, by small groups of architects in different countries throughout Latin America. The architectural merit of the projects included in this chapter lies in the imaginative interpretation of economic,

HOUSE AND STUDIO OF LUIS BARRAGÁN, TACUBAYA, MEXICO CITY, MEXICO.
VIEW OF ONE OF THE ROOF TERRACES.

CASA GILARDI, MEXICO CITY, MEXICO, LUIS BARRAGÁN. VIEW OF THE SWIM-
MING POOL AND THE DINING AREA.

technological, physical, cultural factors that architects carry out in order to pursue typological experimentation. Considering the continually changing nature of these projects, the social housing schemes studied in this chapter challenge traditional methods of historicisation which require buildings not to change – or not to be changed by users – in order to be classified historically. As discussed above, transformation also disrupts the authority of the architect as the sole 'creator' of buildings and obfuscates the historical archiving of a finished work. That is why the buildings presented in this chapter undermine the methods of architectural critique that had been used to uphold their dispossession.

Chapter 5, 'The Private House', presents an overview of singe-family houses in different parts of Latin America. Against the background of poverty brought forward in the previous three chapters, this part re-enters a more familiar territory. Here the analysis of case studies is more heavily determined by form and physical context than by socio-political and cultural factors. The location of the projects – in the Andes, the Argentine Pampa, on the Atlantic and Pacific coasts, on the banks of rivers and the shores of lakes – draws attention to the variety of landscapes of Latin America and the challenges they present to architects, a theme which is continued in the final section of the book. At the same time, the houses examined in this chapter, most of which are holiday retreats, reveal the dramatic fragmentation of Latin American societies and the ever increasing gap between the wealthier and the deprived members of such societies. Some case studies show that contemporary architects frequently undertake commissions in neighbouring countries. The two

houses designed by Chilean architect Mathias Klotz, for example, are built in Uruguay and Argentina respectively, while one of the projects designed by the young Argentine architect Nicolás Campodonico is located in Uruguay. As mentioned above, the transcendence of national borders is a recent development in Latin American architecture, the result of continental trade agreements and international cooperation between countries, treaties that were implemented, or revaluated, in the 1980s.

The final chapter, 'Architectures in Latin American Land-scapes', continues to explore more traditional building typologies: hotels, educational facilities and exhibition spaces. As with the previous section, the analysis of case studies focuses primarily on the form of buildings. However, I have tried to emphasise how, in most cases, the form of buildings derives from sophisticated interpretations of specific landscapes, interpretations based on careful anthropological, cultural and historical studies, not simply on the physical context. The buildings reviewed in this section demonstrate the ability of contemporary architects in Latin America to carry out exciting formal explorations with great environmental concern.

Admittedly, the book does not do justice to its title in the sense that it fails to cover the entirety of Latin America. Not only is Latin America a vast and imprecise region but, more importantly, socio-political and economic conditions (read poverty) make it difficult for architects in many countries to disseminate their work, or for national associations to contribute to such dissemination. Sadly, there is very little information available about architectures in Central American countries like Honduras, Nicaragua or El Salvador. Not much is available about recent architecture in Cuba, although it was a leading centre of architectural development in the 1960s and 1970s. Bolivia is another country whose architecture remains in relative obscurity. It is not that 'exemplary' buildings are not produced in those countries, but that they have not been inscribed in the 'history of architecture'. My admission to their absence from this book is a way to reiterate my belief that the conspicuously singular history of architecture is incomplete and to urge the writing of the missing chapters in that history. Aware of this, and to prevent generalisation, the subtitle of this book refers to contemporary architecture 'in' Latin America. This seemingly insignificant grammatical detail guarantees greater analytical precision. That way, the book refers to buildings that were built there, in Latin America, by architects who are from there too. Yet, it is not implied that the buildings included in this volume represent the architecture of the entire region or that they embody the characteristics of a single and homogenous 'Latin American architecture'. Quite the opposite, focusing on buildings produced in the past ten years, the aim of the book is to show not simply the variety of architectural practices but, also, the vibrancy of the architectural environment in different parts of Latin America and, so, to overcome the deceitful homogeneity expressed in the literature about the modernist masters.

1 Rogelio Salmona received the Alvar Aalto Medal in 2003. The Mexican firm Higuera + Sanchez won the Golden Lion at the 2006 Venice Architectural Biennial and Alejandro Aravena received the Silver Lion at the next edition in 2008. Solano Benitez won the BSI Swiss Architectural Award in 2008. José Cruz Ovalle won the Spirit of Nature Wood Architecture Award in 2008 after winning the Bienal Iberoamericana de Arquitectura y Urbanismo in 2004, a prize which Colombian architect Giancarlo Mazzanti also received in 2008 along with the first prize at Bienal Panamericana de Arquitectura. Angelo Bucci and his team received second place at the 2008 Holcim Award. Yet, the most renowned of all was the Pritzker Prize given to Paulo Mendes da Rocha in 2006 – an honour that he shares with two other Latin American architects: Luis Barragán (1980) and Oscar Niemeyer (1988).

2 The first sentence of *Brazil's Modern Architecture* reads: 'Brazilian architecture is famous, but it is a fame that rests upon the work of a few architects – Oscar Niemeyer, Lucio Costa, Affonso Reidy and one or two others – built in the mid-20th century'. See Andreoli, E. and A. Forty (eds.) *Brazil's Modern Architecture*. London: Phaidon, 2004, p. 8.

3 See Fraser, V., *Building the New World: Studies in the Modern Architecture of Latin America 1930 – 1960*. London/New York: Verso, 2000, p. 88.

4 See Fraser, V.,.*Building the New World: Studies in the Modern Architecture of Latin America 1930 – 1960*. London/New York: Verso, 2000, p. 2.

5 See Holston, J., *The Modernist City: An Anthropological Critique of Brasilia*, Chicago/London: The University of Chicago Press, 1989.

6 Holston criticises the fact that the *rodoviária* has been transformed by its daily users into a place of unusual characteristics: simultaneously a transport interchange, a market place and a town square. For Holston, a transport interchange can neither replace the functions of a market place nor can it serve as a town square. Consequently, rather than positive popular appropriations of the space of the *rodoviária* are seen negatively: they undermine the principles of modern architecture.

7 See the statement for the inclusion of Brasilia in the World Heritage List published by UNESCO. See UNESCO, World Heritage List No. 445, 1987.

8 See Anderson, B., *Imagined Communities: Reflections on the Origin and Spread of Nationalism*. London/New York: Verso, 1983.

9 Fraser, V., *Building the New World: Studies in the Modern Architecture of Latin America 1930 – 1960*. London/New York: Verso, 2000, p. 195.

10 A previous monograph had been written by Sibyl Moholy-Nagy in 1964; however, as P. Villanueva points out, it was written before C. R. Villanueva had completed all his major projects. See Villanueva, P., *Carlos Raúl Villanueva*. Sevilla: Tanais, 2000. – English edition: *Carlos Raúl Villanueva*, Basel: Birkhäuser, 2000.

11 Fraser, V., *Building the New World: Studies in the Modern Architecture of Latin America 1930 – 1960*. London/New York: Verso, 2000, p. 15.

12 All my comments and quotations are taken from the third edition published in the year 2000. The titles of some chapters were changed, and new chapters were added, in this expanded edition published initially in 1996 and re-printed in 1997, 1999 and 2000.

13 Curtis, W. J. R., *Modern Architecture since 1900*. London: Phaidon, (1982) 2000, p. 491.

14 Curtis, W. J. R., *Modern Architecture since 1900*. London: Phaidon, (1982) 2000. p. 493.

15 Curtis, W. J. R.,. *Modern Architecture since 1900*. London: Phaidon, (1982) 2000, p. 567.

16 Curtis, W. J. R., *Modern Architecture since 1900*. London: Phaidon, (1982) 2000, p. 635. This chapter was not included in the first edition but was added later.

17 See Pratt, M. L., *Imperial Eyes: Travel Writing and Transculturation*. London: Routledge, 1992.

18 Small budgets prevent exhilarating formal explorations and the use of advanced technologies which, in traditional architectural terms, leads to the production of boring buildings.

SANTO DOMINGO LIBRARY, MEDELLÍN, COLOMBIA, GIANCARLO MAZZANTI. SOUTH ELEVATION, SEEN FROM PUBLIC PLATFORM.

2 BUILDING ON THE CITY'S EDGE

As discussed above, the rapid growth of Latin American cities in the middle of the 20th century generated numerous urban and architectural problems. Part of those problems was the formation of poor settlements – favelas, invasiones, barrios, etc. – often located on the peripheries of large urban centres. Paradoxically, this happened at a time when the economies of most Latin American countries were thriving due to the post-war crisis in Europe. Consequently, it is not that poverty increased dramatically during this period of time, as is often believed, but that its presence was felt more strongly due to its concentration in cities. In response, a multitude of programmes were devised by national governments throughout the continent in order to eliminate the effects of poverty. During the 1960s and 1970s so-called 'eradication' programmes were implemented in countries such as Brazil, Chile, Colombia, Ecuador, Peru and Venezuela. These plans consisted mainly of eliminating poor settlements by relocating their inhabitants in planned neighbourhoods on the outskirts.[1] As I will emphasise throughout this chapter, these programmes eradicated the poor but not poverty: the causes of poverty were not addressed. It was merely a question of visibility: the image of poverty needed to be concealed. Alarmingly, architects seem to have been complicit with those governmental strategies, as many of the master plans that they designed during the 1940s, 1950s and 1960s demonstrate.[2]

In recent years, however, architects have developed new methods for dealing with the effects that poverty has on the urban morphology of cities throughout Latin America. The buildings examined in this chapter show some of those methods. Rather than concealing poverty, these buildings exalt its existence as an intrinsic characteristic of Latin American cities, an aspect that needs to be tackled directly. Contemporary architects no longer expect their buildings to provide all-encompassing solutions for the problems of cities and neighbourhoods. Though they are bold architectural statements, the buildings reviewed in this chapter address a limited set of socio-political issues specific to the communities who use

FDE SCHOOL IN JARDIM ATALIBA LEONEL, SÃO PAULO, BRAZIL, ANGELO BUCCI AND ALVARO PUNTONI. GENERAL VIEW.

them. These buildings also present a common characteristic: they introduce greater functional flexibility in oder to allow for alternative activities to be held in them, activities different from those specified in the programme (i.e. communal meetings or simply birthday parties). It is, therefore, not surprising that the three architects (or practices) whose buildings are shown in this chapter coincide in their aspiration to use architecture as a means to stimulate social interaction: they want their buildings to become centres of social activity rather than simply schools or libraries. For that reason, I will appropriate the notion of the 'contact zone' from Mary Louise Pratt in order to illustrate the way architects aspire their buildings to operate socially.[3] I find this notion applicable because, rather than harmonious encounters, contact zones are areas of conflict and irresolution where cultural differences are constantly negotiated, though not necessarily resolved. In that sense, the buildings shown in this chapter coincide with the notion of the contact zone both literally and metaphorically. The mere presence of these buildings (and parks) reveals a tension between contrast-

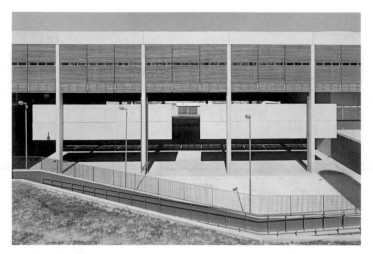

FDE SCHOOL IN JARDIM ATALIBA LEONEL. BACK ELEVATION AND COURTYARD.

FDE SCHOOL IN JARDIM ATALIBA LEONEL. SPORTS GROUND AND COMMUNAL AREA.

ing architectures – those produced by architects and those produced by common people without professional assistance. Moreover, if the aspirations of the architects realise themselves, the buildings will become the setting where local residents will meet either to attempt to negotiate differences or simply to perform that very difference in their daily activities. In sum, more than merely fulfilling a specific function, these buildings are thought to become places of socio-cultural negotiation for the poor in various Latin American cities. Such an attitude removes the priority given to 'form and function' and places an emphasis on the social dimension of architecture where users assume a central role in the production of architectural significance.

Each one of the six buildings examined in this chapter is a punctual insertion into the convoluted urban fabric of informal settlements (slums). Although all are modest in scale, the buildings differ from one another in form, materiality and in the way architects have tackled the relationship between the building and its site. These buildings are examples of a renewed interest in Latin America to improve the conditions of life in poor settlements through the insertion of small and medium size structures which provide facilities needed by local communities. It is important to note that this is only a sample of an increasing number of similar buildings throughout the continent.

FDE School in Jardim Ataliba Leonel | SÃO PAULO, BRAZIL
Angelo Bucci, Alvaro Puntoni

The public school designed in 2004 by Angelo Bucci and Alvaro Puntoni in Jardim Ataliba Leonel, on the periphery of São Paulo, is an outstanding example of this new tendency. The project was commissioned by the Fundação para o Desenvolvimento da Educação (Foundation for the Development of Education) with the aim of creating a 'model' for the construction of other schools in the city. The model needed to be flexible because each possible location had different physical conditions and, also, because functional requirements could vary from case to case. Schools should also allow other activities to be held in addition to their educational main use. Needless to say, rapid construction was another important determinant.

Jardim Ataliba Leonel is a dense and relatively deprived residential area on the northern edge of São Paulo. Although there are a few four-storey social housing blocks, the area is mostly made up of single houses which have been built by the occupants themselves. In spite of the high density, there are neither parks nor public spaces equipped for recreation and for interaction of the inhabitants of the area. Consequently, the school was to become, and in fact has become, a focal point

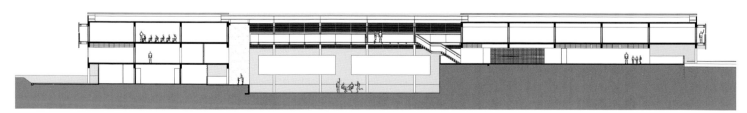

FDE SCHOOL IN JARDIM ATALIBA LEONEL. LONGITUDINAL SECTION.

FDE SCHOOL IN JARDIM ATALIBA LEONEL. NIGHT VIEW OF THE SPORTS GROUND AND COMMUNAL AREA.

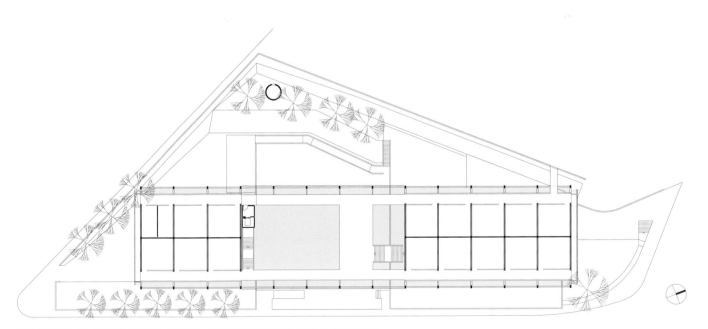

FDE SCHOOL IN JARDIM ATALIBA LEONEL. FIRST FLOOR PLAN: THE CLASSROOMS.

GERARDO MOLINA SCHOOL. AERIAL VIEW.

GERARDO MOLINA SCHOOL. VIEW OF THE CLASSROOM VOLUMES PROTRUDING ABOVE THE CIRCULATION.

for the residents of Jardim Ataliba Leonel, not only visually but also socially and culturally. Therefore, the challenge was to conceive the school not simply as an educational facility in traditional terms but, more importantly, as the only public space in the area.

While its location on a hill was advantageous, it also presented a number of challenges. On the one hand, the hill offered possibilities to enjoy magnificent views over the valley below. On the other, the steep slope meant that multiple levels had to be negotiated in order to guarantee accessibility through the entire school. The latter challenge was successfully resolved by dividing the ground floor into three levels. The higher end of the long rectangular volume provides entrance to the students. They arrive at a partially covered platform that opens to the west and looks down into the multi-sports ground. Passing through a narrow passage, between two service volumes, one finds an external platform in the east. The northern end of the building provides access for the school's staff and houses the administration quarters. The space between these two levels has been sunk to meet the street that runs along the building on the west side. This lower level consists of a multi-sports ground that doubles as a social space for community gatherings on weekends and during the holiday breaks. That is why, at this level, the school symbolically meets the city.

All the classrooms are on a single floor that floats above the multi-level ground floor. The circulations have been arranged around the perimeter so that they contribute to control the incidence of sunlight into the classrooms and offices. In turn, the entire first floor (which contains the classrooms) serves as protection for the sports/community hall on ground level. The perimeter corridors also guarantee a permanent visual link between interior and exterior, allowing students (and users in general) to have different views of their surroundings. To help

attenuate the incidence of sunlight and rain, a series of wooden louvres are embedded in the middle of the concrete frame. Not only do the louvres protect the interior from the elements but, also, emphasise the structural rigour of the composition.

The structure appears to continue a long Brazilian tradition of concrete building, long spans and bridges (although ramps, which were also common in Brazilian modern architecture, are absent from this project).[4] The main structural frame is made of prefabricated concrete elements and metal beams which are articulated in a way that reveals the methods of construction. Internal partitions were kept to a minimum and exterior walls were avoided wherever possible in order to allow for visual transparency and cross ventilation. The intention was that the structure would double as enclosure while being exposed both on the interior as well as the exterior. Concrete elements, metal beams and wooden louvres have been articulated in such a way that they perpetuate themes and formal gestures that appear to be traditional in modern Brazilian architecture but which have also been reinterpreted in order to respond to a significantly less predominant site – on a poor peripheral, highly neglected and, at times, violent, settlement.

In spite of its formal simplicity, the building has a monumental character. It is substantially larger in scale than any other surrounding building, a fact which has turned the school into a landmark in the area and, also, into a centre of social interaction.

Gerardo Molina School | BOGOTÁ, COLOMBIA
Giancarlo Mazzanti

Colombian architect Giancarlo Mazzanti dealt with similar conditions in Bogotá, where he built the Gerardo Molina School in 2008, a building situated in a rapidly growing area on the north-

GERARDO MOLINA SCHOOL. AUDITORIUM AND MULTI-FUNCTIONAL ROOM.

western periphery of the city. As is usually the case in this kind of settlements, the area is densely built with self-constructed adjacent houses. There is little homogeneity in the neighbourhood because houses grow intermittently depending on the fluctuating income of each family – there is no labour stability among the residents of the area, so most families do not have regular earnings. The size of the existing houses varies from one to five storeys. There are also a few social housing blocks in the vicinity which contribute further to increasing population density. Although the programme given by the organisers of the competition called for the design of a school, there were numerous secondary demands, some of which were not included in the brief itself but arose after careful analysis of the site. For that reason, Mazzanti approached the design as if it were an urban

planning project (rather than simply an isolated building) whose main purpose was to endow the growing neighbourhood with social, cultural and recreational facilities for the community, a complex which included a school or, else, which emerged out of the school brief. The architect saw the project as an opportunity to create what I have called a contact zone. In short, the school was designed to become a social space for the community in general rather than a traditional fortified school building which would repel people other than students.

To achieve this, the school was conceived as a continuous winding ribbon whose main elements, the classrooms, twist in response to the surrounding contexts, i.e. it curves inwards where the exiting streets meet perpendicularly the outer boundary of the school and outwards reaching towards existing

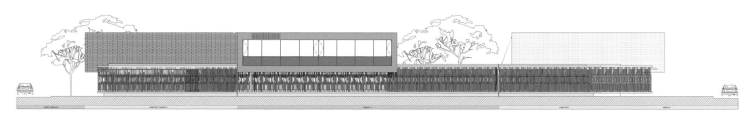

GERARDO MOLINA SCHOOL. SOUTH ELEVATION.

constructions across the street. That way the building creates a variety of external spaces, public parks and squares that can be used permanently by the public, while simultaneously generating a heterogeneous courtyard inside the school for the use of students. Thus, the school generates spaces of different qualities: some are small, others are big; some are open while others are secluded, and this variety facilitates a multitude of public and private activities to take place.

Not dissimilar from the work of other famous Colombian modernist architects, such as Rogelio Salmona, the main functional areas of the programme (classrooms, offices, auditorium, etc.) take rectangular volumes which are distributed on the site and connected by a continuous covered circulation, whose roof is lower than that of the volumes. However, unlike Salmona whose courtyards adhered to a strict preconceived geometry – perfect squares or circles – Mazzanti's design responds to the irregularity of the existing context. The circulation, then, absorbs the apparent disorderly distribution of classrooms, making the entire composition look non-linear and more dynamic. The main difference between Mazzanti's choice of materials and that of other Colombian modernist architects is the lack of brick as main cladding material. Instead, Mazzanti uses stone for the external cladding of the main volumes. Like brick, this natural material is durable and requires little maintenance. It also adds a corrugated texture with variations in tone and colour. Apart from his use of stone, a common material amongst younger architects in Colombia, Mazzanti works with basic traditional materials: concrete, metal, wood and glass.

GERARDO MOLINA SCHOOL. CORRIDORS AND RAMPS TO UPPER-LEVEL CLASSROOMS.

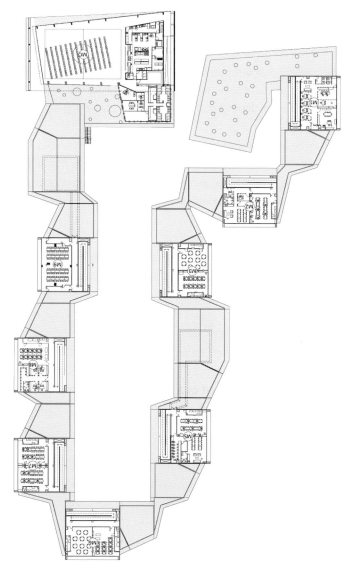

GERARDO MOLINA SCHOOL. FIRST FLOOR PLAN.

A number of level variations, ramps, stairs and leaning columns contribute to exacerbate the vitality of the composition. Furthermore, irregular wooden trellises delimit the circulation (and the rest of building at floor level), permitting a visual link with the surrounding context. Trellises also cast shadows that change during the day, reinforcing the sense of dynamism in conjunction with the winding circulation and the varying height of roofs.

The largest volume of the building is positioned on the north-western corner of the school, facing a currently un-built site reserved for a park. The volume contains an auditorium and other multi-functional rooms which open towards the park and could be used for any activity being held there. Alternatively, the auditorium could be used by local residents for social gatherings. This volume appears to be the physical link between the school and the community.

Working in complex socio-political circumstances has become one of Giancarlo Mazzanti's specialities. In the process, he has perfected what could be called a personal design strategy consisting of protuberant volumes which are articulated by a circulation system with a roof lower than the volumes.

Separate volumes, containing the main programmatic areas, are independent from one another so that each can respond to specific circumstances (i.e. function, views, sunlight, etc.). As a result of the fragmentation of the building's main functions into separate volumes, the entire building – the sum of the volumes and the circulation system – can respond to various aspects simultaneously and in different ways. He has applied this design strategy to two libraries built on the north-eastern hills of Medellín, a very complex socio-political and topographic context. During the 1980s and through most of the 1990s, Medellín was associated with crime. It was, virtually and literally, a war zone. Statistics placed the city amongst the most dangerous urban centres in the world. The average life span of a male citizen in the poor peripheral neighbourhoods was estimated at 17, making the rate of mortality in the whole metropolitan region exceedingly high.

The two libraries are part of a city-wide programme called Red de Bibliotecas Públicas de Medellín (Public Library Network of Medellín). The network comprises an increasing number of interconnected libraries throughout the city.[5] More importantly, the majority of the network's libraries are located in deprived areas of the city, some of which were virtually inaccessible ten years ago due to violence. The main target of the programme is to offer educational and recreational opportunities for local children and young people. To that end, the programme developed the concept of the 'library-park', which consists of multi-purpose library buildings (book collections, auditoria, teaching rooms, etc.) surrounded by public spaces for general use by local residents.

LEÓN DE GREIFF LIBRARY, MEDELLÍN, COLOMBIA, GIANCARLO MAZZANTI. AERIAL VIEW.

León de Greiff Library | MEDELLÍN, COLOMBIA
Giancarlo Mazzanti

The León de Greiff Library, built in 2007 and also known by the locals as Parque Biblioteca La Ladera (Hillside Park Library), sits on the grounds of an old prison, Cárcel de La Ladera, approximately 1.5 kilometres away from the city centre and on the very borderline between the (official) city and the spontaneous peripheral settlements on the eastern hills. This way, the library fits the notion of the contact zone: an interstitial space between diverse and antagonistic social groups. As has become characteristic in Mazzanti's work, the library consists of three two-storey volumes which rest on a plinth. The latter, in this case, is recessed to give the impression that the three volumes float above the surrounding park. Each volume houses a specific function. The southernmost volume, nearer to the entrance, is designed as a community centre containing meeting rooms, a gym and counselling facilities. The central volume accommodates the main library with its own reception, catalogue area, the collection, and reading rooms. The northernmost volume contains the auditorium. It is farther away from the entrance because it is mainly used by organised groups and requires the most security and control.

Connecting the three volumes is a double-high curved circulation space sandwiched between the retaining wall on the east and the three volumes on the west. Near the entrance, on the eastern side, there is a narrow rectangular volume that contains the offices, reception/cloakroom and toilets. As one passes the entrance area, the circulation becomes wider to make room for an exhibition area, a café, two sunken gardens

LEÓN DE GREIFF LIBRARY. THE LIBRARY VOLUMES WITH THEIR VARYING ORIENTATION SEEM TO FLOAT OVER THE HILL.

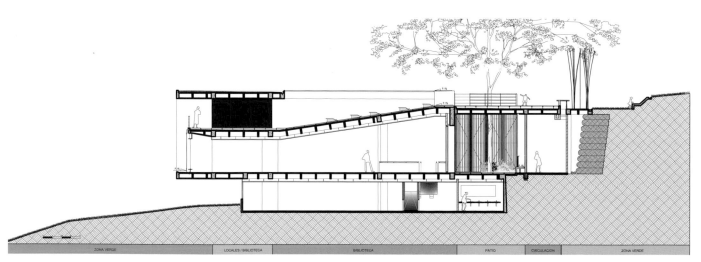

LEÓN DE GREIFF LIBRARY. CROSS SECTION.

LEÓN DE GREIFF LIBRARY. VIEW FROM THE BALCONY.

LEÓN DE GREIFF LIBRARY. RECEPTION AREA.

and, even, an area spontaneously dedicated to nursery at the end of the circulation. Despite its location, embedded between a landmass and the building, the multi-functional circulation space is naturally lit and ventilated and, also, has panoramic views of the city. In turn, the roof of the circulation forms an external public space above the library that serves as a continuous viewing platform to observe the city below and the hills behind. It also provides access to three outdoor theatres on the roof of each volume. In the original design, the public platform integrated a number of existing recreational facilities – a swimming pool, various multi-purpose playing fields and green areas – at the back of the library. Unfortunately, this part of the project has not been completed.

Taking advantage of its position on high ground, each volume is orientated towards a different aspect of the city. The southern volume, which houses the community space, is aimed towards the Plaza de Botero, in the old centre of the city, a square surrounded by various important buildings such as the Palacio de la Cultura and the Museo de Antioquia. The central volume also has a view of the city centre and the western hills across the valley. In turn, the northernmost volume is positioned parallel to the river, looking towards the southwest, and so gaining magnificent views of the entire Aburrá valley.

Santo Domingo Library | MEDELLÍN, COLOMBIA
Giancarlo Mazzanti

The second library designed by Mazzanti in Medellín in 2007 is, arguably, his most successful project to date and, certainly, the most controversial. The Santo Domingo Library, also known as

Biblioteca España, for it was inaugurated by the king of Spain, is located on the eastern hills towards the north of the city. Although accessible by road, the main way to get to the library is by cable car, known locally as Metro Cable. The cable car system was implemented by the local authority in order to gain access to the higher and steeper parts of the peripheral hills which could not be reached either by bus or metro. Approaching the Santo Domingo Library is, therefore, a dramatic experience. It requires a 2-kilometre ride on the Metro Cable hanging at an average altitude of 20 metres over a densely built informal settlement, a squatter settlement which became permanent over the years.

SANTO DOMINGO LIBRARY, MEDELLÍN, COLOMBIA, GIANCARLO MAZZANTI. AERIAL VIEW.

SANTO DOMINGO LIBRARY. VIEW FROM THE PLAZA.

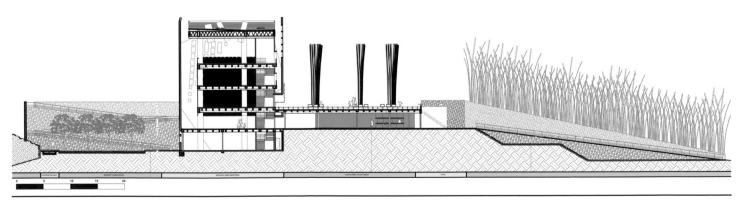

SANTO DOMINGO LIBRARY. CROSS SECTION.

SANTO DOMINGO LIBRARY. VIEW FROM THE SETTLEMENT.

The library sits on a narrow, and very steep, residue plot near the top of the hill. The architectural heterogeneity of the surrounding context, and its convoluted urban fabric, almost precluded a standard solution. Instead, the site demanded a structure that reflected its physical and social complexity while, simultaneously, becoming a recognisable entity for local residents and the city alike.

In Mazzanti's own design tradition, the building consists of three separate volumes united by a circulation platform at ground and lower-ground levels. As in other projects, Mazzanti assigned a specific function to each volume. In this case, the southernmost volume contains an auditorium. Although this can be accessed directly from the public deck, its main entrance is from the covered plaza at lower ground level (directly below the public deck). The central volume is a multi-level library. It has three double-high reading rooms topped by a multi-purpose room on the seventh floor. This is the highest volume and can

be accessed at ground level (public deck), although the main entrance is also at lower ground (covered plaza) opposite the reception space. The northernmost volume is a community centre which contains the offices in the basement, nursery at lower ground level, classrooms and community rooms in the middle two levels and a multi-functional space at the top. The circulation strategy is very similar to the one used in his previous library, it is compressed between the eastern retaining wall and the volumes distributed along the west side. Although it is a continuous space, the width of the covered plaza at lower ground level varies in order to demarcate different areas and to create transitions between them. The gaps between the volumes allow for intermittent views of Medellín as users move along the space. The roof of the circulation provides a public space for the community as well as a viewing platform to observe the city below. However, the urban connection between the library and the existing fabric does not appear to

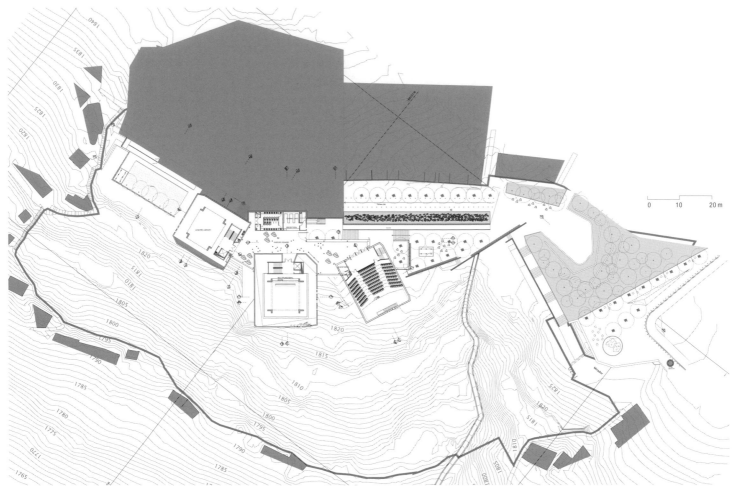

SANTO DOMINGO LIBRARY. SITE AND GROUND FLOOR PLAN.

SANTO DOMINGO LIBRARY. INTERIOR VIEW: REFERENCE COLLECTION.

SANTO DOMINGO LIBRARY. INTERIOR VIEW: READING ROOM.

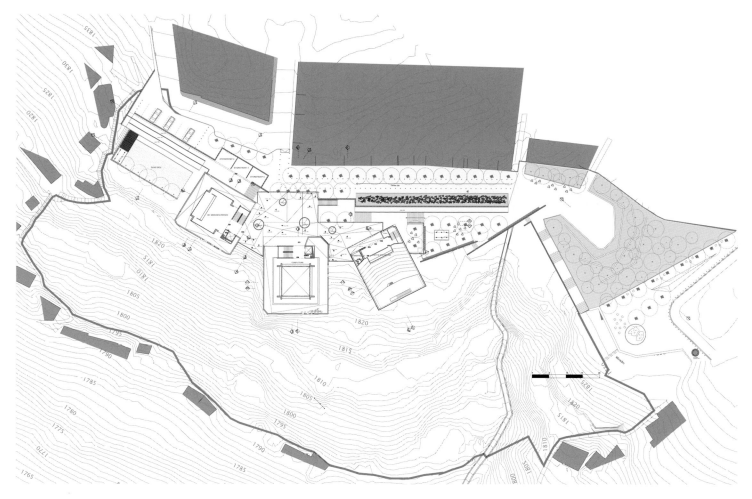

SANTO DOMINGO LIBRARY. FIRST FLOOR PLAN.

be fully resolved at the moment. The main pedestrian access from the south and the link with the adjacent street that runs along the east side of the library appear to be somewhat weak. This could be due to the fact that external works usually get the least amount of budgetary attention. This may only be a temporary flaw. At present, a new pedestrian bridge is being built to grant access from the low end (south-west) and the axis linking the Metro Cable station with the library is also undergoing reconstruction. Such changes will prompt the completion of the public space around the library and its connection with the surrounding areas.

Considering its difficult location, and the socio-political ambitions it represents, the Santo Domingo Library is a magnificent building. In fact, Mazzanti won the prize for best building at the Bienal Iberoamericana de Arquitectura held in Portugal in 2008 and later that year received the First Prize at the Bienal Panamericana de Arquitectura in Ecuador. Curiously, the project only received a honorific mention in the XXI Bienal Colombiana

de Arquitectura (2008). In addition to the numerous accolades, the most remarkable achievement is the success it has had amongst the local community who speak with pride about their new library and cultural centre. I would like to suggest that, in fact, this is the main architectural value of the building. The Santo Domingo Library has accomplished its aim of becoming a centre of social activity and a strong image, which, along with a number of other projects in the area, has transformed a highly violent and virtually inaccessible shanty town into a more hospitable neighbourhood.

Metro Cable | CARACAS, VENEZUELA
Urban Think Tank

Caracas is another Latin American city that has experienced an accelerated growth in the past 50 years. Before World War II, Caracas was, in Latin American terms, a relatively small city with less than a million inhabitants. Today, however, the popula-

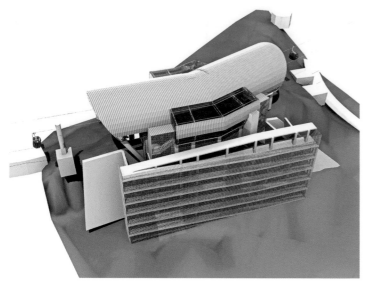

METRO CABLE, CARACAS, VENEZUELA, URBAN THINK TANK. VISUALISATION OF ONE OF THE STATION BUILDINGS.

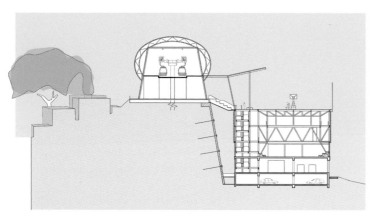

METRO CABLE. SECTION OF STATION BUILDING.

tion of the metropolitan area exceeds six million people. Like in other Latin American cities, such a dramatic growth caused the development of numerous informal settlements in and around the city's original core. The main characteristic of these settlements was their lack of infrastructure: roads, transport, services (water, power, etc.) as well as a lack of provision for education, recreation, health and social care.

As mentioned earlier, the first reaction in most Latin American countries was to eradicate informal settlements by providing mass social housing in other parts of the city's periphery. However, provision for education, recreation, health and social care was poor – sometimes inexistent – on the newly expanded peripheries. In fact, such facilities were often situated in the city centres and people needed to travel long distances to reach them. As a result, there was not only great

physical fragmentation but, also, increasing socio-political isolation. More importantly, the socio-political tension that arose from such fragmentation materialised itself in disapproval of the governments' plans and, also, in violence. The buildings that we have analysed so far in this chapter are the result of a different approach to the challenges presented by densely occupied informal settlements. These kind of projects have been described by many theorists as 'articulators',[6] spaces which attempt to reconnect fragments of the city that have become separated and, in that way, facilitate the flow of goods, people, vehicles and capital. It is, therefore, not accurate to suggest that these buildings are a purely architectural initiative, they result of larger political programmes. Their architectural significance lies in the fact that they focus on the micro-politics of place rather than the homogenising macro-politics of the modernist plans implemented throughout the 20th century.

The work of the Urban Think Tank (U-TT), led by Alfredo Brillembourg and Hubert Klumpner, adheres to this position. They started their research practice in 1998 and have studied the development of informal settlements in Caracas for over ten years. Many of their projects are the result of workshops attended by residents of the city's slums. They claim to design in response to people's needs as well as in response to their specific conditions of habitation (physical, social and economic). Usually projects are fully designed before the architects have signed a contract with the government. In spite of working in an inverse manner (opposite to the way most architectural practices operate) in the past five years, Brillembourg and Klumpner have been able to realise a few of their proposals for Caracas' poor areas.

Their project for the Metro Cable from 2009 shares many similarities with its counterpart in Medellín. The Caracas Metro Cable is designed to facilitate access to San Agustín del Sur, a hilly area that developed on the south bank of the river and which is abruptly separated from the city centre by the *autopista* (highway) that crosses the city from east to west, parallel to the river. At present, there is limited access for vehicles; cars can only reach some areas at the lower end of the hilly sector. Instead of streets, San Agustín has a complex network of pedestrian narrow pathways leading to the higher parts of the settlement. In spite of its precarious urban conditions, San Agustín sits on a privileged location. It borders the botanic gardens and the famous campus of the Universidad Central designed by Carlos Raúl Villanueva, both on the west. The infamous *helicoide*, the National Intelligence Headquarters,[7] lies on the east end of the hill chain. The northern slopes of San Agustín have magnificent views over Caracas, an urban landscape dominated by the presence of the Torres del Parque

METRO CABLE. STATION BUILDING IN CONTEXT OF EL MAGUITO QUARTER.

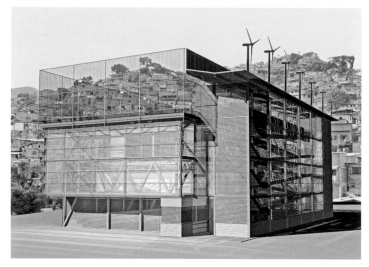

VERTICAL GYM, CARACAS, VENEZUELA, URBAN THINK TANK. VISUALISATION OF THE BUILDING IN CONTEXT.

VERTICAL GYM. SPORTS FACILITIES IN A DENSE URBAN FABRIC.

Central, a 1970s high-rise development which includes two of the tallest towers in Latin America.

As it does in Medellín, the Caracas Metro Cable will operate as a branch of the metro reconnecting San Agustín with the rest of the city through its mass transport system. It is expected that the Metro Cable will also bring visitors from other parts of the city to enjoy the new amenities and the views from the top – as has happened in Medellín and São Paulo where similar elevated transport systems are already in operation. Each station of the Caracas Metro Cable will have an additional specific function. One will be a rehearsal centre for young musicians, part of the successful Fundación del Estado para el Sistema de Orquestas Juveniles e Infantiles de Venezuela (State Foundation for the Venezuelan System of Juvenile and Children Orchestras). One will be a 'vertical gym' (also a concept advanced by U-TT). The top station will be surrounded by a viewing platform and ample spaces for leisure and social interaction. This way, an infrastructural project is transformed into a focus of urban revitalisation.

To achieve this, the gondolas of the cable car have been calculated to transport cargo (up to 800 kilogrammes per gondola) during the off-peak hours. This will allow local residents to bring in goods, construction materials and so on to their properties in the upper parts of the hill. At the same time, the Metro Cable will provide opportunities for local residents to create small industries at home because they will be able to take their products out of San Agustín for trading. An anecdote that deserves mention is that, due to the density of the area, the construction process has required a combination of high-tech construction methods and manual labour. The foundations for the masts, for example, were dug by hand with shovels while the masts themselves were prefabricated and brought to site by helicopter.

Vertical Gym | CARACAS, VENEZUELA
Urban Think Tank

Another exemplary project developed by Alfredo Brillembourg and Hubert Klumpner's U-TT is the Vertical Gym, a typology that results from the need to build 'upwards' in dense areas where vacant sites are both rare and extremely small. Rearticulating creative ideas from multiple case studies (i.e. hotel gyms in tall buildings and ingenious popular solutions to make football pitches on steep hills in the barrios of Caracas), Brillembourg and Klumpner have developed a prototype for a multi-layered sports facility that could be built in the hilly slums of Caracas. Although there is only one vertical gym currently operational,

VERTICAL GYM. INTERIOR OF MULTI-SPORTS HALL.

a few more are under construction. Due to the density of the urban fabric, vertical gyms are not designed to have a striking exterior image; they are often occluded by the surrounding buildings. Instead, they are conceived to be experienced from inside. The quality of interior space, rather than their image, is essential to produce a sense of comfort that invites people to stay and play sports. In order to reduce the cost of maintenance, the architects have explored possibilities to make the gyms sustainable and self-sufficient. The prototypes, designed to be built in traditional materials such as concrete blocks and metal trusses, also incorporate wind turbines and photovoltaic cells as a way to make the project financially and socially viable. It will be interesting to see how this seemingly appropriate new typology evolves, once the vertical gyms are operational.

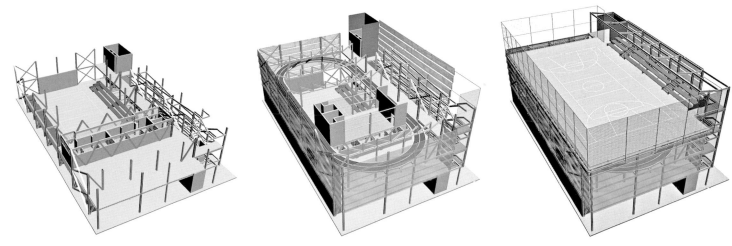

VERTICAL GYM. AXONOMETRIC VIEW OF DIFFERENT LEVELS.

1   See Hernández, F., P. Kellet and L. Allen, *Rethinking the Informal City: Critical Perspectives from Latin America*. Oxford/New York: Berghahn Books, 2009. Essays in this book discuss extensively the history and long-lasting effects of eradication programmes in Latin American cities.

2   See, for example, the plans designed by Town Planning Associates (José Luis Sert and Paul Lester Wiener) in Rovira, J. *José Luis Sert: 1902–1983*. Barcelona: Electa, 2003.

3   See Pratt, M. L., *Imperial Eyes: Travel Writing and Transculturation*. London: Routledge, 1992.

4   See, for example, João Batista Vilanova Artigas's School of Architecture at the University of São Paulo, FAU-USP, Affonso Eduardo Reidy's Museum of Modern Art in Rio de Janeiro, or Lina Bo Bardi's São Paulo Art Museum.

5   There are five libraries currently in operation. Yet, in 2008, there was a competition for two more libraries expected to be built in 2009/2010.

6   See Fiori, J. and Z. Brandão, 'Spatial Strategies and Urban Social Policy: Urbanism and Poverty Reduction in the Favelas of Rio de Janeiro' in *Rethinking the Informal City: Critical Perspectives from Latin Amer-*

ica edited by Hernández, F., P. Kellett and L. Allen. Oxford/New York: Berghahn Books, 2009.

7   The *helicoide* is an extraordinarily large building which occupies an entire hill in the middle of the city. It was conceived as the largest cultural and commercial centre in Venezuela. However, the project was never fully completed, nor was it fully occupied. Today, the building serves as headquarters for the National Intelligence Service.

PARQUE DEL AGUA, BUCARAMANGA, COLOMBIA, LORENZO CASTRO. VIEW OF WATER COURSES.

3 PUBLIC SPACES AS CONTACT ZONES

I have used the concept of the contact zone in order to describe one aspect that appears to be central in the agenda of many contemporary architects in Latin America: people. Interestingly, the foregrounding of the social dimension of architecture, as seen in the projects examined so far, has not prevented architects from carrying out intriguing formal explorations. On the contrary, careful analysis of the complicated socio-cultural and political conditions, as well as the difficult economic environment within which Latin American architects work, has prompted a multiplicity of themes which, in turn, stimulate a diversity of formal searches. More important, however, is the fact that, while formally appealing, the projects examined in the previous chapter were conceived deliberately in order to be subverted by users. The three architects (or practices) whose work was documented are at pains to underline that they inevitably design buildings on the basis of certain prevalent ideologies – mostly aesthetic but, also, technical, functional, etc. – which are not necessarily significant or intelligible for the user. Hence, by encouraging users to appropriate their buildings, they expect their very architectural aspirations to be challenged.

The notion of the contact zone, then, appears to be fitting for various reasons. On the one hand, buildings emerge as brief and transitory points where two separate and distant assemblages overlap: architecture and people. More literally, the notion of the contact zone suitably illustrates the fact that buildings provide physical spaces where people meet and interact permanently. However, buildings are not expected to resolve, in its entirety, the problems of the people they are addressed to. As explained in each of the case studies above, buildings can only resolve directly a limited number of problems, mostly those associated with their programme, i.e. education, recreation and transport. However, by providing additional communal spaces, these buildings create opportunities for people to meet and attend to other matters regarding the community. Not without a certain naivety, the architects included in the previous chapter describe enthusiastically that, in addition to football matches

AVENIDA 24 DE MAYO, QUITO, ECUADOR, DIEGO AND LUIS OLEAS. AERIAL VIEW AT NIGHT.

and Sunday afternoon feasts, they expect political gatherings to take place and community councils to be held in their buildings. The case to argue is that, if their optimistic expectations realise themselves, then buildings will not be the setting of harmonious resolution but, on the contrary, a place where socio-political tensions and cultural differences will both become visible and be enacted. For, as Mary Louise Pratt reminds us, contact zones are sites of struggle rather than unruffled consensus.

Like the previous six case studies, the following five projects help to make visible an emergent set of aspirations, a change in attitude towards the practice of architecture amongst a young generation of architects in Latin America who are interested in designing for the people without forgoing their position as designers. Although the five projects studied in this section differ greatly in scale, function and location, they coincide in disproving theories according to which the only way to activate public space is through retail. In fact, it could be argued that the five projects consist of removing excessive commerce in order to stimulate alternative ways of social interaction. Equally

PLAZA DE SAN VICTORINO, BOGOTÁ, COLOMBIA, LORENZO CASTRO.
AERIAL VIEW.

PLAZA DE SAN VICTORINO. VIEW TOWARDS THE *CORDILLERA*.

transport and urban infrastructure. Part of the plan was designed by Rogelio Salmona, Colombia's most famous architect, who pedestrianised a long stretch of the Avenida Jiménez. Other architects produced plans for a number of public spaces including the Parque Tercer Milenio and the Hospital de San José Square. Thus, San Victorino Square is only the latest of a series of projects in the area, all of great architectural merit.

Lorenzo Castro's project of 1998 proposed the partial pedestrianisation of three of the four streets which surround the square. That way, existing retail venues could be integrated with the square uninterrupted by passing vehicles, which now can only circulate along the western edge of the square, though at reduced speed; the streets on the east and south sides are devoted to pedestrians only. Avenida Jiménez, on the northern edge of the square, remains a viaduct for heavy traffic. Yet, it was slightly altered in order to integrate a station of the city's new mass transport system: Transmilenio.

Remarkable for its simplicity, the square consists of three clearly demarcated sectors: a mixed or semi-hard area consisting of a concrete-slab floor finish with scattered trees on the east; a hard area (brick floor finish) in the middle of the square crossed diagonally by a stream of water; and a slightly elevated garden area on the west. This spatial arrangement responds successfully to the circulation of pedestrians and to the local environmental conditions. Considering that most historical and cultural attractions – as well as the city's administrative buildings – are located only three blocks away from the square towards the east, it is expected that most visitors will arrive from and depart in that direction. Hence, the concrete floor finish on the semi-hard area enters the square as a continuation of the pavement directing people in and out of the square. The scat-

PLAZA DE SAN VICTORINO. INITIAL SKETCH.

PLAZA DE SAN VICTORINO. THE SQUARE IS ANIMATED BY A WATER COURSE.

tered trees on that sector of the square provide protection from the mild morning sun but permit easy access and circulation of people. The central area of the square consists of an open space that lends itself to multiple uses, i.e. itinerary markets, streets vendors, *ludo* players or bird feeders – activities which could easily extend to the previously described zone. The green area on the west has larger trees which provide shelter from the strong afternoon sun. The semi-elevated garden area is surrounded by an assortment of benches, an attraction that has proven to be irresistible to the high number of newspaper readers. The square, however, is not flat. A modified topography helps to emphasise the three mentioned areas while, at the same time, generating a multitude of smaller spaces within the square which are creatively appropriated by users: children like to play in the water, intellectuals read the paper or play board games on the benches around the trees, others simply offer their wares or skateboard along the edges of the low walls.

Parque del Agua | BUCARAMANGA, COLOMBIA
Lorenzo Castro

The sobriety and geometrical simplicity of the San Victorino Square is a far cry from the Parque del Agua (Water Park) that Lorenzo Castro designed in 2004 in Bucaramanga. With this project Castro won the National Architecture Award at the XIX Bienal Colombiana de Arquitectura (2004) and the First Prize at the XIV Bienal Panamericana de Quito the same year.

Bucaramanga is a much smaller city than Bogotá with a rugged topography and exuberant vegetation. Rather than an urban square, this was a large-scale intervention on the northeastern edge of the city. The aim of the project was to turn the city's water treatment plant into a public park where visitors could recreate while learning about the purification processes of water.

The project proposes a series of wide pedestrian circulations which articulate the different parts of the treatment plant. Embedded in the circulation network are small spaces surrounded by water and protected by dense vegetation. These secluded niches form a separate system of tranquil spaces in

PARQUE DEL AGUA, BUCARAMANGA, COLOMBIA, LORENZO CASTRO. MAIN PEDESTRIAN CIRCULATION.

PARQUE DEL AGUA. PERIPHERAL PEDESTRIAN CIRCULATION.

PARQUE DEL AGUA. SECONDARY PEDESTRIAN CIRCULATION, BENCHES AND VEGETATION.

PARQUE DEL AGUA. ARTICULATION OF LEVELS AND MATERIALS.

PARQUE DEL AGUA. LAYERING OF DIFFERENT MATERIALS IN ELEVATION.

opposition to the dynamism of the pedestrian paths which are animated both by people and by water cascading along the sides.

Taking advantage of the rugged topography, Castro proposes an interesting play of distant and close views. Certain areas of the circulation open up to allow passers-by to see large portions of the park and, in places, the city behind. This also provides an opportunity for walkers to orientate themselves in what otherwise could be described as a maze. Other parts of the park are treated as enclosed and inward-looking corners where visitors are encouraged to focus on specific details: a tree, a wall, a cascade.

The material palette of the whole project is vast. Stone appears to be dominant as both cladding and floor finish. Concrete is left bare in many parts of the park where it works as retaining wall, floor finish or simply as furniture. Brick is also present throughout the park and is used as floor finish and to make the walls of minor structures (kiosks and service booths). Wood is used for benches, tables and fences, and, also, as a contrasting organic material against a mostly mineral palette. Needless to say, water was considered as yet another material:

an element that introduces vitality and dynamism into the park. Castro masterfully articulates such a variety of materials by layering them – mostly in elevation. That way, each material reveals its function and contributes to dramatise the perspective – or the way people understand space through perspective.

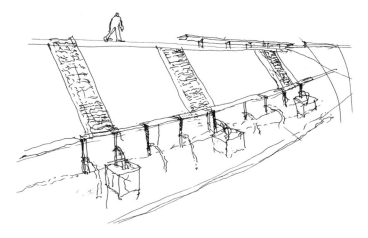

PARQUE DEL AGUA. SKETCH OF PEDESTRIAN CIRCULATION.

PARQUE DEL AGUA. DIALOGUE BETWEEN NATURAL AND ARTIFICIAL MATERIALS.

PARQUE DEL AGUA. MAIN PEDESTRIAN CIRCULATION AND LOCAL VEGETATION.

As with the previous case, San Victorino Square, Castro refuses to introduce functions that determine use. Instead, in the Water Park, he proposes a system of paths which connect a series of non-functional spaces, each different from the other in form and in materiality. Thus, Castro leaves it up to users to decide how they want to appropriate space. Variations of scale, materials and ambience are his way of multiplying the possibilities for people to use the park. Such an approach to design allows the architect to display his or her creative ability without imposing specific functions on people. There is an interesting act of dissociation between form and function and, at the same time, an intention to reinforce the link between architecture and people.

Parque de los Deseos | MEDELLÍN, COLOMBIA
Felipe Uribe de Bedout

There is great affinity between the public spaces designed by Lorenzo Castro and the themes that Felipe Uribe de Bedout explores in his 2003 design for the public space that surrounds the Planetario Municipal Jesús Emilio Ramírez (Municipal Observatory) and the adjacent Edificio de la Música (Music Rehearsal Centre) in Medellín. In fact, the latter building was also designed by Uribe de Bedout, and, so, the two interventions are generally presented together. The site is located in a complicated area approximately 2 kilometres north of the city centre, a contact zone between the historic core and vast areas of urban sprawl which developed rapidly in the 1960s and 1970s towards the north of Medellín. In addition to the clash between different urban morphologies, the site is flanked by three major public buildings: the campus of the Universidad de Antioquia, the botanic gardens and the Municipal Observatory. The three,

however, were disarticulated and contributed to the perceived lack of order in the area. Of course, the problem was not only morphological. The great socio-political instability of the 1980s and 1990s had an enormous effect on areas where people from different economic strata met. Insecurity and vandalism drove the observatory, the botanic gardens and, even, the university to consider relocation. However, a series of urban interventions at the end of the 1990s – including a stop of the metro at the university – prevented the closure of the three institutions and helped to reconstitute the area.[2]

The Music Rehearsal Centre aligns itself with the Municipal Observatory forming a diagonal across the entire block. The building is elevated above the ground to permit the transit of

PARQUE DE LOS DESEOS, MEDELLÍN, COLOMBIA, FELIPE URIBE DE BEDOUT. VIEW OF EDIFICIO DE LA MÚSICA.

PARQUE DE LOS DESEOS. GENERAL VIEW OF THE PLAZA WITH EDIFICIO DE LA MÚSICA (RIGHT) AND MUNICIPAL OBSERVATORY (LEFT).

people beneath it. In the upper levels, the building provides spaces for children and young musicians to rehearse. The ground level was conceived as a covered square with a series of food stalls that serve mainly university students and nearby office workers. These commercial outlets help to guarantee activity in the square throughout the day.

The large windowless southern façade of the observatory was transformed into a screen, while the northern façade of the music building was designed as a 'projection booth' which doubles as a stage. That way, images and videos can be projected upon the external wall of the observatory or, alternatively, musicians can perform to people on the plaza, events which happen regularly throughout the year. Thus, the open plaza between

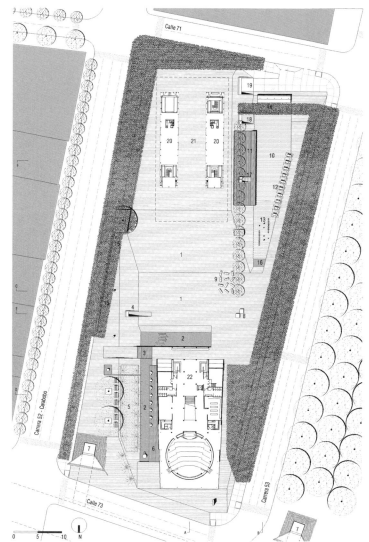

PARQUE DE LOS DESEOS. GENERAL SITE PLAN.

PARQUE DE LOS DESEOS. VIEW OF EDIFICIO DE LA MÚSICA AND FOUNTAIN.

PARQUE DE LOS DESEOS. CINEMA PROJECTION FROM THE EDIFICIO DE LA MÚSICA WITH PEOPLE SITTING ON THE PLAZA.

PARQUE DE LOS DESEOS. ROTATING BEDS/BENCHES ON THE PLAZA.

the two buildings is treated as a terrain that allows people to sit, or lay, and enjoy the shows. Indeed the name of the project, Parque de los Deseos, derives from the possibility to lie on the ground at night to observe the stars and make wishes.

The diagonal alignment of buildings creates a series of triangular spaces, each of which has different characteristics. There is a shallow reflecting pond on the north-eastern side which invites people to take their shoes off and walk in the water. The south-western corner offers a more secluded space

that is frequently visited by couples of students. The northern-most tip has turned into a social hub due to the metro station and the proximity of other public facilities such as the botanic gardens and the Parque Explora.[3] The Parque de los Deseos is furnished with creatively designed bed/benches, table/lamp-posts and other devices which fulfil multiple functions and invite users to appropriate them. In sum, the main idea behind this architectural intervention is that people are the signifiers of public space.

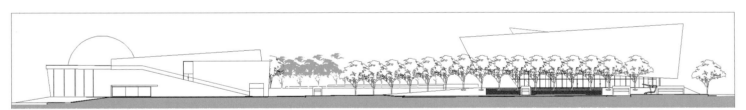

PARQUE DE LOS DESEOS. LONGITUDINAL SECTION ALONG THE WESTERN EDGE OF THE PLAZA.

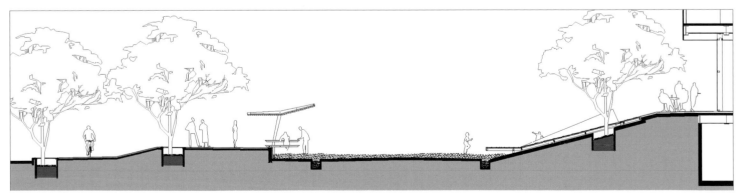

PARQUE DE LOS DESEOS. DETAILED SECTION OF PLAZA ON THE EAST SIDE OF THE EDIFICIO DE LA MÚSICA.

PASEO COSTA, ANFITEATRO COSTA, BUENOS AIRES, ARGENTINA, CLAUDIO VEKSTEIN. OUTDOOR THEATRE STAGE AND ACOUSTIC SHELL.

Paseo Costa | BUENOS AIRES, ARGENTINA
Claudio Vekstein

In slightly similar conditions, the Argentine architect Claudio Vekstein took the challenge of designing a longitudinal park along the shore of the River Plate in Buenos Aires, realised in 2000. The municipality had proposed to recuperate a stretch of the river's edge which had fallen into disrepair and to regain 18 hectares of land from the river for recreational purposes. The site required architects to deal with two heavily polluted streams of water which flow into the River Plate at the southern end of the proposed park.

Vekstein's proposal for stages three and four of the project[4] consisted of a series of terraces which start at the north end and descend towards the south where an open-air theatre is built on a peninsula-like area formed at the point where the two polluted water streams reach the river. In order to negotiate the varying levels between the terraces, which descend from west to east (toward the river), and from north to south (in the same direction as the river flows), Vekstein created a series of artificial beaches – made of refined debris produced during the construction of the park and taken also from other nearby construction sites – which are separated by patches of endemic vegetation. Both the beaches and the vegetation prevent the river bank from eroding, specially during the rainy season floods.

A series of pedestrian circulations connect the linear promenade on the west edge of the park with the river shore. The promenade – which has differentiated lanes for vehicles, bicycles and pedestrians – contains services and public facilities such as restaurants, cafés, public toilets and parking for vehicles, most of which were designed by Vekstein. In turn, pedestrian paths help to negotiate the complex arrangement of varying levels between terraces. However, this causes the paths visually to disappear in the changing topography. To correct this effect, Vekstein designed a lamp post which is used to light all pedestrian circulations in the park. Ambiguously, to the viewer, the lamp posts seem to emerge out of the ground so that only the posts can be seen but not the paths. Only at night, when they glow, do the lamp posts fully serve their purpose, revealing the position of the paths, and, also, their angular shape. In keeping with the geometry of the lamp post, or vice versa, pathways are not perpendicular to the promenade. Instead, they are rotated in different angles directing the views of passers-by towards the tidal River Plate which, in this part of Buenos Aires, is approximately 45 kilometres wide. Hence, as

PASEO COSTA, ANFITEATRO COSTA. OUTDOOR THEATRE STAGE AND SITTING AREA WITH THE CITY IN THE BACKGROUND.

PASEO COSTA, ANFITEATRO COSTA. THEATRE IN USE DURING THE SUMMER SEASON.

PASEO COSTA, ANFITEATRO COSTA. STAGE AND ACOUSTIC SHELL AT NIGHT.

Vekstein puts it, views are always the same, yet different. This is true in the sense that the river is always in the horizon, but some paths focus on the islands up the river (to the north), or on the port and the centre of Buenos Aires south of the park. Paths also vary in size and in form as a way to introduce a different experience each time people take a different route.

The two most dominant architectural features of the park are the monument to the Argentine architect Amancio Williams,

on the north end, and the amphitheatre Costa on the south end of the park. The monument was originally designed by Williams himself as a monument to his father, the musician Alberto Williams. It was built originally in 1966 as an exhibition pavilion to celebrate the centenary of the Sociedad Rural de Argentina in Palermo (not in Buenos Aires). Although it was demolished only two months after completion, the pavilion became a representative piece of Argentine modern architecture. The reconstruction of the project, to commemorate ten years of the architect's death, was a collective endeavour carried out with the participation of family members of Alberto and Amancio Williams, the archaeologist Marcelo Wiessel, architect Claudio Vekstein and architecture students from the nearby Torcuato di Tella University.

The monument consists of two concrete columns that support two concrete canopies approximately 15 metres above the ground, resembling two gigantic palm trees. The canopies, which do not touch, are placed diagonally to each other. The distance between the adjacent corners is projected on the ground to form a square pond virtually connecting the two

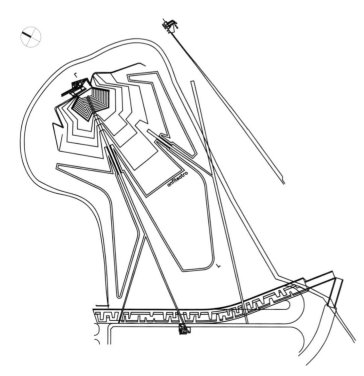

PASEO COSTA, ANFITEATRO COSTA. PLAN OF OUTDOOR THEATRE STAGE AND SEATING AREA.

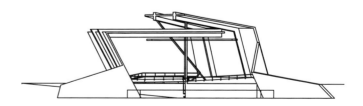

PASEO COSTA, ANFITEATRO COSTA. WEST ELEVATION OF OUTDOOR THEATRE STAGE AND ACOUSTIC SHELL.

PASEO COSTA, MONUMENT TO AMANCIO WILLIAMS. THE MONUMENT FORMS AN ICONIC IMAGE.

PASEO COSTA, MONUMENT TO AMANCIO WILLIAMS. SITE PLAN.

canopies. The pond serves as the centre of a larger square area demarcated by benches. In turn, the benches, which do not touch either, extend centrifugally in all four directions, visually extending into the park while permitting the park to enter into the monument. Although distant from the main promenade and, hence, standing in relative isolation, the presence of the towers has a powerful effect, especially at night, when a carefully planned lighting arrangement dramatises the slenderness of the columns and the audacity of the cantilevers.

At the opposite end of the park, near the south entrance, is the Anfiteatro Costa which occupies an area of approximately 6 hectares. It is designed for a capacity that varies between 1,500 (sitting) and 30,000 people. Using the stage as a centre, and continuing with the compositional theme of the park, the amphitheatre responds to a series of concentric trapezoid terraces continuing the same geometry used throughout the park. In fact, in plan, the amphitheatre and its surrounding terraces appear to be a magnified version of the northern terraces which are smaller in size. The stage was designed to be a visually attractive piece, so as to counteract the monument to Williams at the other end of the park. It is conceived as a skewed

arch whose generous dimensions result from programmatic demands (a multi-functional open-air theatre and concert place). The stage is made of concrete and the arch (which doubles as flying tower for theatre acts) is made of metal. Ancillary func-

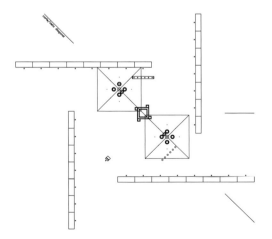

PASEO COSTA, MONUMENT TO AMANCIO WILLIAMS. PLAN SHOWING SITTING ARRANGEMENT AND LIGHTING.

tions (toilets, changing and rehearsal rooms, deposits, etc.) are tucked under the stage.

While fulfilling the intention of becoming a visually attractive element in the park, the stage appears to be somewhat convoluted. Some of its components seem to be oversized, and there is an exaggerated amount of gestures and features in addition to the acoustic and lighting paraphernalia required for it to operate successfully. As a result, the intended dynamism of the composition becomes dissipated, and the amphitheatre loses a great deal of its architectural strength; an issue stressed by the fact that this part of the park has suffered greatly from vandalism and decay.

The latter point brings us back to an earlier discussion regarding the relation between architecture and people, for it is interesting to note that the most successful areas of the Paseo Costa designed by Claudio Vekstein are the intermediate terraces without buildings. It is common to see people reading, sunbathing, playing games on the grass or simply walking along the park. These areas are used continually by locals and visitors alike throughout the year but, especially, during the summer months. The lack of specific function makes the small area around the monument to Williams another favourite point for visitors (in spite of its current state of deterioration). On the other hand, the southernmost terrace of the park, where the amphitheatre is located, appears to be less attractive to users; although it is used heavily during the theatre season. It could be argued that the specificity of its function – the sitting arrangement, for example – precludes appropriation and becomes a deterrent for people who, out of the theatre season, only want to spend some time in the park. One might maintain, however, that vandalism is a form of popular appropriation and, so, the amphitheatre has, indeed, been appropriated by the public. In fact, such acts of violent appropriation of architecture by users reflect the clash between the aspirations of the architect – and the municipality, in this case – and the expectations of the people.

The increasing interest in the design of public spaces in various countries throughout the continent is indicative of a sig-nificant change in the way architects and authorities approach the growth of Latin American cities. It has been explained how the governments of the 1960s, 1970s and 1980s implemented programmes to eradicate poverty. The majority of these programmes consisted of the removal of poor people from city centres, or nearby areas, and their relocation to the outskirts. In other words, the poor were eradicated but not poverty or its causes. On the contrary, such programmes contributed to accelerate the expansion and fragmentation of cities as well as to obstruct economic and social development at community level.

In place of these inadequate programmes, architects (as well as authorities and other professionals involved in the design of cities) in Latin America have developed methods of urban intervention whose aim is to improve, rather than replace, existing conditions of life in poor areas of cities. As shown in the last two chapters, this is achieved both via the insertion of complementary facilities such as schools, libraries and community centres as well as by exploring the potential of public space – parks, squares and pedestrian routes – to encourage social interaction. The advantage of this kind of punctual intervention is manifold. First of all, it reduces substantially the cost of the projects, which no longer require demolition and replacement of existing structures. Second, it minimises the impact of construction both on the city and on the specific areas where plans are being implemented (because interventions are much smaller in scale). More importantly, they do not disturb the functioning of local communities – the economies and social dynamics that have developed spontaneously through the years – but intend to complement them.

What the projects in this chapter – and the following – show, is not a change in the way architects appropriate contemporary Euro-American architectures (as discussed in the introduction), but in the way these architectures are implemented to the greater benefit of particular communities in specific cities throughout Latin America. The following chapter exposes the way in which the same generation of young architects tackles another problematic architectural theme: social housing.

1   The project was not built entirely as the architects had planned because the contract did not include supervision of the construction work.

2   I mention the metro simply because, according to recent studies, its construction marked a pivotal point in the stunning recuperation of Medellín.

3   The Parque Explora, designed by Alejandro Echeverri Restrepo, is another outstanding building in this part of the city.

4   The project was designed and built in various stages over a period of seven years and with the participation of other architectural teams and landscape designers.

TEATINA-QUINCHA SHELTER, PISCO, PERU, ALEXIA LEÓN.

4 DESIGNING FOR POVERTY

The provision of social housing in Latin America became a pressing issue during the first half of the 20th century. This was a period when most capital cities, as well as other major conurbations, doubled and, even, tripled in size due to the emergence of a precarious industrialisation. As a result, during the 1940s through to the 1960s, Latin American governments began to promote the construction of large social housing projects in order to accommodate a rapidly growing population.

Paradoxically, many famous architects preferred not to become involved in the design of this kind of schemes. Oscar Niemeyer and Luis Barragán, for example, believed that the bureaucratisation of social housing was an impediment for the realisation of 'good' architecture, an attitude which generated irate reactions in certain quarters, especially from those working in academia. Amongst those who felt uncomfortable with such attitudes was Alfonso Eduardo Reidy, who criticised some of his contemporary Brazilian colleagues for being indifferent to the problem of social housing. He pointed out that the large concentration of poor people in peripheral and inner-city slums was having an increasingly negative effect on the fabric of cities like Rio de Janeiro and São Paulo – as well as on their socio-political administration. Thus, Reidy called for Brazilian architects to participate actively in the provision of social and low-income housing; unfortunately his call did not have great resonance amongst his colleagues.

However, if the interest and economic support of central governments led to the construction of numerous projects in Brazil and other Latin American countries, the fact that the buildings were not designed by famous architects has led to a significant absence of examples of social housing from the literature about Latin American modernism. Amongst the few exceptions are three remarkable projects: the Pedregulho Housing Complex in Rio de Janeiro (1950–1952) by Affonso Eduardo Reidy, as well as El Paraíso (1952–1954) and Urbanización 23 de Enero (1955–1957) by Carlos Raúl Villanueva in Caracas. Following the principles of the CIAM, these projects

QUINTA MONROY, IQUIQUE, CHILE, ELEMENTAL – ALEJANDRO ARAVENA. HOUSES AFTER OCCUPATION

included schools, markets, health centres, as well as community rooms and recreational facilities in addition to accommodation. The grandiloquence of these three projects embodies the architectural optimism of the era, and the architects' firm belief in modernist narratives of progress and universalisation. The schedules of accommodation represent an extreme rationalisation of society and impose patterns of behaviour whose aim is the optimisation of economic productivity. People – particularly the poor – were taken as an undifferentiated mass. Indeed, the expression 'mass housing', often used to describe projects of social housing, gives evidence of the way in which the poor were approached, both by governments and by many architects, namely as a homogenous body. Therefore, it is possible to affirm that the above-mentioned projects were conceived for an 'imagined community' – to use Benedict Anderson's term – which did not correspond with the realities of poor people in Caracas and Rio de Janeiro, but with an idealised version of 'people' that represented the nationalist and 'progressivist' agendas imposed by most governments throughout the continent. Anderson's term, imagined community, appears to be fitting.in this depiction of the socio-political ethos

QUINTA MONROY. HOUSES BEFORE OCCUPATION.

of mid-20th-century Latin America. In his book, he maintains that nation, nationality and nationalism are entities difficult to define; the terms themselves are imprecise. Thus, he argues that the suitable definition for a nation is an imagined community represented largely by its institutions (its language, laws, boundaries, government and so on) rather than by the homogeneity of its peoples. Consequently, in constructing the nation as an imagined, historically homogenous body, the *concept* of nation erases the heterogeneity of its citizens. In other words, the concept of nation occludes the existence of social, cultural, ethnic, religious, class and other forms of difference amongst the people, the constituents of the nation.[1]

The projects examined in this chapter demonstrate that many aspects of the homogenising attitudes found in the era of nationalism have changed considerably. After half a century of experience and research, contemporary architects – as well as planners and the authorities concerned – have developed alternative strategies of dealing with the provision of social and low-income housing which correspond more accurately with the fluctuating socio-political and economic circumstances in each Latin American nation. Another aspect architects are beginning to come to terms with is the existence of cultural

differences, and the way these are performed both collectively and individually. Here and in previous chapters, I have used the term 'cultural difference' along the postcolonial critic Homi Bhabha in order to acknowledge the coexistence of multiple subject positions within the space of the nation, all those positions which the concept of nation itself occludes under the cloak of an imagined community. As the term itself suggests, cultural difference does not attempt to eliminate difference. On the contrary it brings it forward, makes it visible and, above all, assigns socio-political validity to the cultural products that result from the interaction between different groups of people. That is why the concept of cultural difference is useful in this discussion about architecture for the poor: it opens up a theoretical space suitable to study the contribution of common peoples in the continuous re-shaping of cities, neighbourhoods and buildings. The purpose of this chapter, therefore, is to illustrate some of the alternative strategies that contemporary architects in Latin American countries employ in order to cater for the existence of cultural difference and, also, to examine the architectures that such strategies generate.

I will start this brief overview of recent social housing projects in Latin America by examining the work of ELEMENTAL, a practice based in Santiago de Chile and led by the architect Alejandro Aravena. Not only is ELEMENTAL an exemplary case because they have built thousands of housing units throughout Chile, they have also developed an innovative approach to low-income housing that is now being employed in other Latin American countries and around the world.

It is not necessary to reiterate at this point that Chilean cities, as others in the rest of Latin America, have experienced an accelerated growth during the past 50 years. However, it is important to stress that, in spite of many similarities, processes of urbanisation were different in each country. To affirm the opposite would be to deny the existence of tremendous socio-political, economic and cultural differences between them. In fact, as the projects examined in this chapter demonstrate, only by understanding the specificities of each particular location can architects respond successfully to the challenges inherent in the provision of social housing. The specificities of location are not only geographical or climatic but, also, social, political, economic and technological. It is precisely because of their ability to engage critically with such a complex set of circumstances that the work of ELEMENTAL is exemplary in the field.

ELEMENTAL attempts to provide middle-income housing to families that are unable to attain such a standard of living and which would be statistically not capable to repay an ordinary mortgage. Working within a governmental framework created in 2001, ELEMENTAL designs housing units with an average budget of US$ 10,000. In order to provide middle-income housing with such a tight budget – rather than complying with minimum standards for low-income housing, which they consider to be unacceptable – ELEMENTAL designs a basic unit that comprises only the kitchen, bathroom and the external walls. This unit is bigger than an ordinary social housing project and is also built with better materials, though it is not finished. The units are designed in such a way that residents can modify and extend their dwellings according to their own needs and their fluctuating income.

This approach to social housing introduces an important political variable to the design of buildings, one by which users are conceived as producers of their own habitable space. The consequence, however, is a dissociation between the author (architect) and the building, as well as between the building and its image, which can no longer be considered immutable. While this approach certainly corresponds more accurately with the swiftly changing socio-political circumstances that surround the lives of the Latin American poor, it also presents a scholarly challenge because existing methods of architectural historicisation are unsuitable to deal with the dynamism inherent in the buildings designed by ELEMENTAL. Hence, in the same

QUINTA MONROY. HOUSES AFTER OCCUPATION.

way that architects have had to develop alternative methods of design to respond to the specific circumstances of the poor, scholars are faced with the need to produce suitable methods to record historically and theorise these new architectures. For the purpose of this publication, drawings (plans, sections and elevations) show the contribution of the architects, while the images illustrate some of the alterations carried out by users, alterations which result in the constitution of vibrant urban landscapes that reveal the heterogeneity of Chilean peoples.

Quinta Monroy | IQUIQUE, CHILE
Alejandro Aravena

One of the first social housing schemes built by ELEMENTAL in 2003 was located in Iquique, a small coastal city approximately 1400 kilometres north of the capital Santiago. The project consists of 93 housing units in a deprived area south of the city centre. The site was occupied by the same people for whom the project was designed. However, the conditions in which they lived were unhealthy, unsafe and overcrowded. For that reason, representatives of the Chile Barrio programme, which sponsored the project, approached the community and offered to subsidise new housing in the same location. Initially, the residents rejected the offer fearing that they were going to be relocated to other parts of the city – as had happened to some of them before. In fact, negotiations broke down and residents had to be evacuated by the police before the construction could commence.

In order to reduce the sense of overcrowding, the new houses are distributed in linear blocks that form ample public spaces in front of the houses. Rather than simply streets, public spaces facilitate social interaction (recreation and commerce)

QUINTA MONROY. INTERIOR BEFORE OCCUPATION.

QUINTA MONROY. INTERIOR AFTER OCCUPATION.

and increase security by means of visibility – residents can see people when they enter the courtyards. The blocks consist of an arrangement of horizontal and vertical modules 6 metres deep by 3 metres wide. The houses on the ground floor occupy three horizontal modules, two of which are built and a third that is left vacant for future development. The ground level forms an urban plinth upon which a second layer of houses is built using a different configuration. The upper level houses occupy only one horizontal module (6 x 3 metres) but are distributed vertically rather than horizontally. As with the units on the lower level, the 3-metre gap between houses is reserved for future development. In the initial arrangement the upper level houses appear as narrow towers resting on a continuous concrete slab supported by the lower level houses, an arrangement that conveys a sense of rhythm and stability. More importantly, this initial configuration contains the structure that permits residents to extend their houses in the future at very low cost. The houses on ground level can grow to an area of 54 square metres (plus a 27-square-metre backyard planned to remain

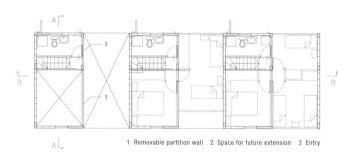

1 Removable partition wall   2 Space for future extension   3 Entry

QUINTA MONROY. SECOND FLOOR PLAN.

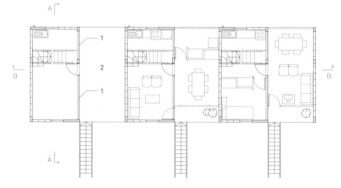

QUINTA MONROY. FIRST FLOOR PLAN.

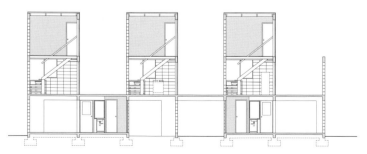

QUINTA MONROY. SECTION B-B.

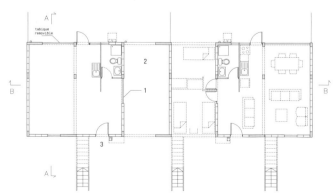

QUINTA MONROY. GROUND FLOOR PLAN.

LO ESPEJO, SANTIAGO DE CHILE, CHILE, ELEMENTAL – ALEJANDRO ARAVENA. HOUSES AFTER OCCUPATION.

undeveloped), while the houses on the upper level can grow to an area of 72 square metres. That way, when completed, the total area of both lower and upper level units would be similar to that of a middle-income residence, exceeding the average area of a low-income house by 18 and 36 square metres respectively. When the houses have grown to occupy all the vacant spaces, the blocks will have solidified, yet their image will not be homogenous; since residents complete their houses according to their own possibilities (and tastes), the result is one of great heterogeneity.

In order to keep costs down, all external walls are made of concrete block, while internal and other moveable partitions are made of wood (chipboard and plywood). Floor plates and structural bracing are made of cast-in-situ concrete while staircases, both external and internal, are made of wood as a temporary measure; residents can replace them later either with concrete or metal.

In spite of the initial reluctance, and the traumatism caused by the temporary displacement to nearby camps, residents returned to occupy their new houses in the place where they used to live and where they had formed a community. The stupendous reception of the new houses by the residents helped to build up confidence in the projects promoted by the Chile Barrio programme and in the ability of ELEMENTAL to produce innovative solutions for low-income housing in other places in Chile.

Lo Espejo | SANTIAGO DE CHILE, CHILE
Alejandro Aravena

In 2005 ELEMENTAL was commissioned by the government to design 30 houses in Lo Espejo, the poorest and most densely populated commune of Santiago's metropolitan area, approximately 12 kilometres south of the city centre. The purpose of the project was to relocate 30 families which lived in an illegal settlement near the assigned site. Initially, the area of the site appeared to be sufficient to build comfortably the required number of houses. However, a restriction prohibited to

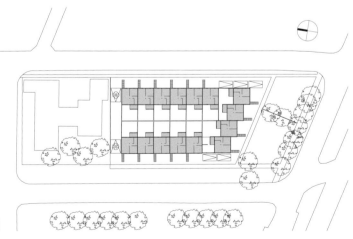

LO ESPEJO. SITE PLAN.

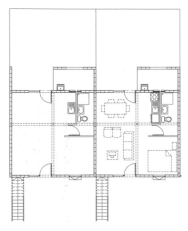

LO ESPEJO. GROUND FLOOR PLAN.

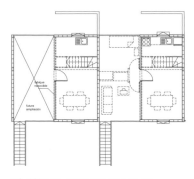

LO ESPEJO. FIRST FLOOR PLAN.

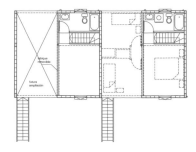

LO ESPEJO. SECOND FLOOR PLAN.

build on a 10-metre fringe along the southernmost end of the site because it had been occupied by a sewage (now decommissioned). Consequently, in order to reduce the total built area, the houses were packed closer to one another at the north end of the site, and the house typology of the previous project had to be slightly modified.

The houses were organised conventionally in three rows around the periphery of the site. On ground level the houses occupy a 6 x 6-metre module with another 36-square-metre module left vacant at the back for future development. The

upper level houses correspond with the typology of the previous project, though a roof covers the whole 6 x 6-metre module in such a way that it forms a continuous plane linking each row of houses together.

Unlike the previous project – where all units can grow unto the adjacent vacant space – in Lo Espejo, only the upper level units can grow into the allocated gap. The lower units, on the other hand, can only expand onto the backyard. However, losing the backyard would cause significant ventilation and lighting problems. It could also cause legal disputes with the

LO ESPEJO. HOUSES BEFORE OCCUPATION.

LO ESPEJO. HOUSES AFTER OCCUPATION.

RENCA, SANTIAGO DE CHILE, CHILE, ELEMENTAL – ALEJANDRO ARAVENA. GENERAL VIEW OF THE COMPLEX BEFORE OCCUPATION.

neighbours in the upper level. To prevent this from happening, it is necessary to regulate the development of the units by imposing controls which would somewhat contradict the idea of free appropriation of space by users. This limitation highlights the inability of a building typology, conceived for a particular site, to satisfy the conditions of another site and the needs of a different group of people. Only the continued study of this project, the monitoring of its changes, will provide clues to optimise the concept for future application; indeed ELEMENTAL is carrying out this study diligently.

Renca | SANTIAGO DE CHILE, CHILE
Alejandro Aravena

This project, also from 2005, consists of 170 housing units in a province situated on the north-east of Santiago's metropolitan area. The site was purchased by the residents of various informal settlements nearby who wanted to improve their living conditions without having to move farther away from the city centre – where most of them work. However, after acquiring the site, it became apparent that it had been used as an illegal

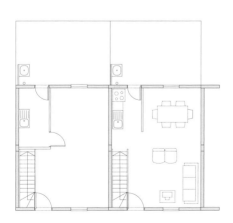

RENCA. GROUND FLOOR PLAN.

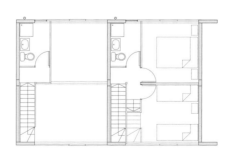

RENCA. FIRST FLOOR PLAN.

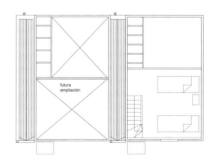

RENCA. SECOND FLOOR PLAN WITH SPACE FOR FUTURE EXTENSION ON THE LOWER LEFT.

RENCA. HOUSES BEFORE OCCUPATION.

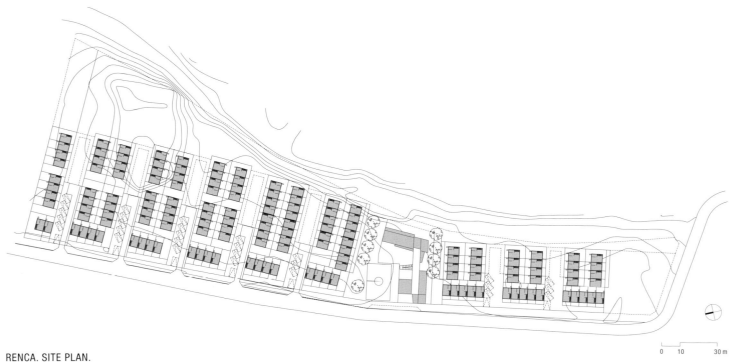

RENCA. SITE PLAN.

RENCA. LAST STAGES OF CONSTRUCTION.

RENCA. INTERIOR BEFORE OCCUPATION.

landfill and, consequently, the mechanical conditions of the soil were not apt for construction. This posed the problem of having to excavate and refill the site, an operation that would increase the cost of construction fourfold. The situation was aggravated by a series of building restrictions: a 16-metre-wide margin was expropriated along the north edge of the property for the construction of a motorway; a pylon supporting high-voltage power lines prevented construction on the east side; on the south the law required the developer to widen the existing road, a condition which added yet another unexpected item to the budget. In order to fit the necessary number of houses in the substantially reduced site, ELEMENTAL proposed a vertical housing system which would minimise greatly the footprint of the project. The system would also reduce the amount of excavation and refilling necessary to make the ground suitable for construction. Rather than catering for both horizontal and vertical expansion, as in the last two projects, the houses in Renca can only grow upwards within a given structural grid of 4.5 metres front by 6 metres in depth by three storeys in height.

The basic house is a three-storey empty volume with a kitchen on ground level and a bathroom on first floor exactly above the kitchen, the remaining area is a 28-square-metre open plan (and a three-storey void). However, the empty volume can be filled gradually by residents, and each house can eventually have three bedrooms and a total built area of 63.4 square metres – the average size of a middle-income house in Chile. This configuration also serves to guarantee three important aspects: 1. that all the hydraulic servicing is installed by specialists, 2. that a suitable structure is provided for the future

development of the house and, 3. to justify the need for stairs in a house that originally has no levels; since the bathroom is strategically located above the kitchen, the stairs that lead up to the bathroom can later become the staircase of the house.

The structural and material palette in Renca is somewhat similar to the previous project. There is a concrete frame with embedded brick walls up to first floor level. A simple wood structure sits on top of the masonry walls supporting the roof and making space for an attic level. Residents do proceed to insert partitions and floors slabs, often using wood boards (plywood and chipboard). Not only is this the most inexpensive way of extending their houses, it also maintains a certain flexibility in case they need to carry out further alterations.

Undoubtedly, Renca is a more accomplished project in terms of urban and house design, a project which demonstrates the continued process of research and reflection carried out by ELEMENTAL for nearly a decade. It could be argued, nonetheless, that the structure imposes limitations on users who can only extend their houses within the confines of an empty volume given to them at the beginning. Yet, the simple fact of conceiving a structure that permits users inexpensively to customise their dwellings according to need, income and taste is a commendable architectural achievement. More importantly, with this strategy ELEMENTAL has been able to transform social housing into an investment opportunity for the poor who, in the past, were banned from the so-called 'property ladder'. Indeed, ELEMENTAL were awarded the Silver Lion at the 2008 Venice Architectural Biennale and have received many other accolades in recognition for their work with poor communities throughout Chile.

URBANIZACIÓN CAÑAVERAL, MEDELLÍN, COLOMBIA, ANA ELVIRA VÉLEZ. GENERAL VIEW OF THE PROJECT AND THE LANDSCAPE OF THE ABURRÁ VALLEY.

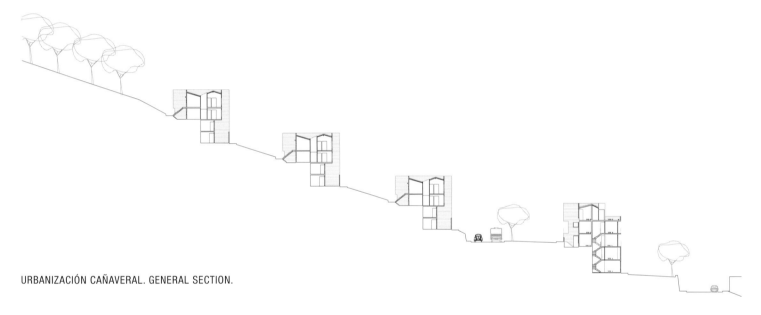

URBANIZACIÓN CAÑAVERAL. GENERAL SECTION.

Urbanización Cañaveral | MEDELLÍN, COLOMBIA
Ana Elvira Vélez

Twentieth-century social housing schemes in Colombia were generally modest in scale compared with others built in Brazil, Mexico and Venezuela (to mention a few countries) during the 1950s. There was also a tendency to favour single-family houses over large multi-storey blocks and, if high densities were necessary, architects would opt for low-rise building clusters instead of towers. But, if the size of the projects designed by Colombian architects were smaller, they shared the interest of carrying out formal and technical explorations with their Latin American counterparts. The projects for La Fundación Cristiana (started in 1963 and never fully completed) and La Palestina (1964) designed by Rogelio Salmona come rapidly to mind. In these projects Salmona undertakes a formal exploration in an attempt to break away from the volumetric poverty always associated with low-income housing. Such an exploration, however, caused building schedules to elapse and costs to increase to the point that both projects became too expensive for the poor. As a result, governmental institutions developed a distrust in the ability of renowned architects to design low-budget schemes. By the end of the 1960s, distrust, and the privatisation of the housing sector, caused architects to lose their power to influ-

URBANIZACIÓN CAÑAVERAL. ACCESS TO THE HOUSES; THE ARRANGEMENT OF BLOCKS IN THE TOPOGRAPHY ALLOWS FOR VIEWS OF THE ABURRÁ VALLEY.

URBANIZACIÓN CAÑAVERAL. TOP FLOOR TERRACES.

ence decisions regarding the provision of low-income housing. This situation remained largely unchanged for 30 years, a period during which many of the country's cities reached advanced stages of deterioration. Towards the end of the 1990s, the government found itself forced to implement comprehensive programmes in order to salvage the damages caused by three decades of abandonment. Such programmes gave architects a renewed opportunity to participate in the development of cities and to correct the shortcomings of past projects. The following case studies show some of the aspects that have become central to the agenda of Colombian architects involved in the provision of social housing today. It is important to note, however, that substantial research on this area has been undertaken at universities across the country and, consequently,

newer alternatives are being produced constantly. Thus, a topic that was considered to be dull by many architects is turning into an exciting area of academic exploration and practice – this applies not only to Colombia and Latin America but also to other countries in the developing world.

The Urbanización Cañaveral, completed in 1998, is a project that embodies recent attempts to improve the formal and spatial characteristics of low-income housing. It is located on the western hills of Medellín, in an area that has developed recently due to the construction of a cable car which connects settlements in the hills with the city's metro system.[2] The steep topography determined the linear alignment of houses in rows that twist slightly in order to accommodate themselves to the contour lines. Not only does this arrangement minimise the amount of excavation necessary to prepare the site, it also maximises the flow of air through the buildings and guarantees that views are not obstructed. As the rows of houses twist with the topography, a series of public areas are formed between them. These have been minimally landscaped with only the necessary pathways, lighting, benches and refuse collection points. The intention is to encourage residents to appropriate these areas by introducing whichever function the community deems necessary. The green areas on the periphery of the site were left untouched in order to allow local vegetation to grow. The communal car park is located on the south-eastern corner of the site, nearer to the road, in order to avoid the cost of building internal streets, as well as to liberate as much area as possible for communal use.

URBANIZACIÓN CAÑAVERAL. FIRST, SECOND AND THIRD FLOOR PLANS.

URBANIZACIÓN LA PLAYA. VIEW OF ONE OF THE BLOCKS FROM THE INTERNAL PUBLIC SPACE.

There are 150 housing units divided in six different types – three types in each of the two stages of construction. Once the position of the six longitudinal blocks had been established, the design team proceeded to subdivide the length of the blocks into plots of 6 x 12 metres. Each plot contains three housing units which are distributed vertically over two or three levels. The units are intricately intertwined in such a way that every apartment has its own entrance, balcony and laundry area. Although the intricacy of the distribution restricts flexibility and impedes the future transformation of the apartments, it introduces an interesting spatial quality that many social housing schemes do not have. It also has an effect on the exterior image of the project, which appears as a regular series of volumes expressed by two different materials: brick and concrete blocks.

Urbanización La Playa | MEDELLÍN, COLOMBIA
Ana Elvira Vélez

Urbanización La Playa, built in 2004, is located in the centre of Medellín, on a site that was left vacant by the demolition of a

textile factory. This marks an important shift in the provision of social housing schemes, which had traditionally been assigned to the outskirts, away from the city centre. As mentioned earlier, the relocation of poor settlements on the peripheries of Latin American cities was a way of creating an image of cleanliness and homogeneity while, simultaneously, protecting the cost of land in areas where large-scale real estate investment was expected. Therefore, this project demonstrates the emergence of new architectural and planning attitudes to tackle both poverty and rapid urban growth in Colombia.

The project sits on a rectangular site of 87 x 90 metres which is surrounded by multi-storey housing on three sides (south, west and east) and by the Quebrada Santa Helena, a small river on the north side. It consists of three rectangular blocks that are parallel to La Playa Avenue on the north side. The five-storey-high blocks are grouped closer to the southern edge of the site in order to create a public space along the avenue. The public space includes a viewing platform on the northernmost corner of the site and a park on the south. In addition to this public space which opens to the street, the zigzagging blocks create two outdoor areas whose scale is six possible permutations of the plan. Apartments also have a small balcony whose position varies for each unit. The changing position of the balconies introduces dynamism to the fenestration of the 68-metre-long façades.

More than vertical circulations, the oblong stairwells are conceived as transitional spaces from public to private. Their form and proportion facilitate interaction between residents and, even, encourage alternative uses. It is not rare to find laundry hung on the stairwells or to see social gatherings spilling outside the apartments onto the generous landings.

The importance of these two projects – which deserved commendation in two Colombian architectural biennials – is that they demonstrate how architects are exploring different strategies to satisfy both housing demands and the specific needs of poor people in Colombia. At the same time architects are trying out, formally and spatially, various ways of transforming the image of social housing; not only the way it looks but, also, the way it is perceived by the public.

Brasil 44 | MEXICO CITY, MEXICO
Higuera + Sanchez

Another example of city-centre low-income housing was designed in the centre of Mexico City by the firm Higuera + Sanchez, which, since 2008, took the name JSa (Javier Sanchez Arquitectura). The project named Brasil 44, completed in 2007, is significantly smaller than the previous examples. It consists of a reinterpretation of the *vecindad*, a very common housing typology in Mexico. The *vecindad* is an urban multi-family tenement with apartments arranged around a central courtyard. Initially, *vecindades* were subdivisions of large single-family courtyard houses. However, in response to the rapid growth of the capital in the early 20th century, *vecindades* began to be purpose-built as a housing option for transitory dwellers – seasonal workers, artisans, etc. – as well as for rural migrants who moved permanently to the city.

URBANIZACIÓN LA PLAYA. VIEW OF ONE OF THE BLOCKS AND THEIR RELATION WITH OTHER BUILDINGS IN THE CONTEXT.

smaller and, hence, are more intimate. They are conceived for the residents rather than the general public.

Initially, the apartments consist of a basic unit measuring 5 x 10.5 metres with a narrow strip of services attached to one of the longer sides (bathroom, the kitchen and a laundry area). The rest of the space is an open plan that can be divided into six different configurations according to the needs and economic capacity of each family. On the façade, each apartment has four identical windows carefully distributed according to the

URBANIZACIÓN LA PLAYA. WEST ELEVATION.

BRASIL 44, MEXICO CITY, MEXICO, HIGUERA + SANCHEZ. ELEVATION FROM BRASIL STREET.

BRASIL 44. VIEW OF THE COURTYARD.

Brasil 44 is located in the historic centre of Mexico City, an area which suffered significant damage in the 1985 series of earthquakes. The project was sponsored by the Mexican Ministry of Housing and Urban Development (SEDUVI) and the Institute of Housing (INVI) in association with the regional government of Andalucía. It is part of a programme that aims to reduce land speculation and to improve conditions of habitation in currently overcrowded tenements. Architects are invited to restore existing *vecindades* which, once completed, are sold to residents who can buy the property with subsidies given by the government.

JSa's proposal consists of restoring the central courtyard to its original dimensions and keeping the existing commercial outlet at the front, a bridal gown shop. Taking advantage of the high ceilings, mezzanine levels were introduced in both floors, thus converting a two-storey structure into a four-level building. The roof was converted into a generous launderette with a small social space.

Every effort was made for the building to retain the two traditional components of a *vecindad*: the courtyard and the *zagúan* – an entry corridor leading from the street to the courtyard. The plans follow a simple distribution of apartments, one on each side of the courtyard with the staircase at the back

between the two. Such a layout makes the courtyard the most prominent space of the building. It serves not only as a lightwell and ventilation area for all the apartments but, also, as a social space that needs to be traversed by residents every time they enter or leave their dwellings. The bridal shop at the front of the building responds to the commercial character of the street which already has other shops of the same kind.

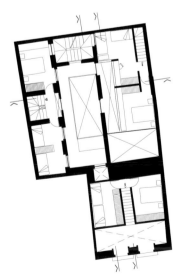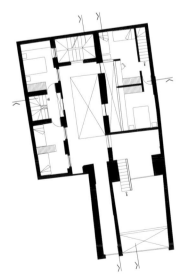

BRASIL 44. FIRST FLOOR PLAN.   MEZZANINE PLAN.

BRASIL 44. VISUALISATION OF THE BUILDING IN ITS CONTEXT.

JSa won the Golden Lion at the 2006 Venice Architectural Biennale in the urban project category for the design of this project and has received multiple other commendations in Mexico. In spite of its formal simplicity and its small scale, the worth of the project lies in the subtle contribution it makes to the recuperation of a deprived area of Mexico City and the sensibility with which the firm undertook the design and restoration of a building typology, the *vecindad*, whose cultural value is often undermined.

Teatina-Quincha Shelter | PISCO, PERU
Alexia León

In order to conclude this brief overview of social and low-income housing in Latin America, I will examine a small but multifaceted structure designed by the Peruvian architect Alexia León. León has dedicated a significant part of her career to study the vast coastal desert region on the south-west of Peru, where she has built most of her projects. The Teatina-Quincha is an emergency shelter for the victims of the magnitude 8.0 earthquake that affected the country in 2007, causing significant damage to the city of Pisco. Unlike other projects in this chapter, this temporary structure, built in 2007–2008, is designed to

last between two to five years. However, it has the potential to expand gradually and, so, to stretch its life span.

In this project León explores an indigenous construction technique known as *quincha*. The name derives from the Quechua language and refers to walls, or fences, made of three materials: bamboo (or cane), woven bark panels (for reinforcement) and mud to cover the structure.[3] Considering that these materials are inexpensive, readily available in the region and, also, that local residents are familiar with their use in construction, León sustains that the *quincha* is an appropriate building technique for both low-income and emergency housing in Peru. What is more, given the flexible properties of these three natural materials, the *quincha* is a seismic-resistant structure.

The form of shelter designed by León was inspired by the *teatina*, which is the name given in Peru to a kind of lightwell and ventilation shaft commonly used in warehouses, industrial buildings and, even, in housing. The *teatina* appeared to be appropriate for this basic emergency shelter because its funnel-like shape facilitates air circulation and allows natural light into the building when the pivoting bamboo shutters are down to close the habitable space.

This way, León articulates an indigenous construction technique, the *quincha*, with an urban solution, the *teatina*, in order to produce an alternative form of accommodation for contemporary Peruvian people. Interestingly, the function of the structure created by León does not correspond with any of its two predecessors, but emerges as something new. Though it retains some of the formal characteristics of both antecedents, the function of the Teatina-Quincha Shelter has been completely re-codified. Indeed, it is possible to describe this case as an example of architectural hybridisation, a term which depicts the continued process of cultural re-articulation that occurs in con-

TEATINA-QUINCHA SHELTER, PISCO, PERU, ALEXIA LEÓN. VIEW OF *TEATINAS* ON THE ROOF OF AN OLD WAREHOUSE.

TEATINA-QUINCHA SHELTER. ERECTION OF BAMBOO STRUCTURE.

ADDITION OF *ESTERAS*, PANELS MADE OF BAMBOO BARK.

ditions of transcultural interaction. Moreover, rather than being merely a combination, or merger, of foreign and local elements, León works with cultural and architectural designations taken from different Peruvian traditions.[4] Not only does this attitude demonstrate that there is a rich coexistence of multiple cultural and architectural traditions within the space of one single nation, Peru (or, else, that Peru is not culturally homogenous), it also shows that Europe and North America have been displaced from their position as dominant referents which determine architectural production in Latin America. Thus, rather than negative, hybridisation is a sign of cultural productivity, as well as a sign of the creativity of Latin American architects.

Another aspect worth mentioning is the potential inherent in the Teatina-Quincha Shelter for dynamic development or, in other words, for the consolidation of a temporary into a permanent structure. Since many of the emergency camps built after the earthquake could become the permanent place of residence for many of the poor victims, León's overall proposal went beyond the mere design of a shelter and became a project of community participation. It considered strategies for the cultivation of bamboo and suggested workshops to teach residents how to build using these materials. In that sense, not only does León's project provide an immediate solution for the victims of future earthquakes, it also encourages the formation of communities of dwellers through the construction of their own dwellings and the gradual consolidation of their settlements. Though it is an exceedingly small and simple structure, the architectural significance of León's project lies in the fact that it connects multiple aspects – technical, formal, historical and socio-political – in the production of a shelter whose initial function can be altered, expanded and re-codified by users. Indeed, it appears to be a common characteristic of many of the

projects studied in this chapter that architects do not conceive buildings as finalised but, on the contrary, as incomplete entities which will be continually (re)created by users. In other words, buildings are conceived under the premise that they will never be completed; they will always remain in the process of being built. Such a condition of performativity – in the way the cultural critic Homi Bhabha uses the term[5] – precludes the straightforward classification of their buildings in terms of 'national' identity, or as part of any given architectural movement.

Although, theoretically, the notion of architectural performativity in social and low-income housing is not new – John F. C. Turner, for example, began to promote his notion of 'self-construction' since the 1970s, though he did not use the same terminology[6] – its widespread implementation is, indeed, both a recent occurrence and a refreshing development. Such an approach to the provision of social housing differs greatly from the attitudes of many 20th-century architects whose schemes required not only physical completion but, also, the adaptation of residents to the dynamics of operation envisioned in the master plan.[7]

Another aspect worth mentioning is the visible reduction in the scale of the projects. The optimism characteristic of the 20th century materialised itself in a long list of immense projects. Entire cities were planned, some were built and multiple projects were put forward for the re-ordering of metropolitan areas and larger regions. In fact, there were architectural and planning practices dedicated almost entirely to designing master plans for Latin American cities. The work that Josep Lluís Sert carried out with the New York based firm Town Planning Associates comes readily to mind. They designed more than 30 master plans for cities in eight different Latin American countries; none of them was fully completed, many never broke

TEATINA-QUINCHA SHELTER. COMPLETED SHELTER, BEFORE COVERING WITH ADOBE.

ground. The cases examined in this chapter give evidence of a substantial reduction in the size and scope of current social housing projects, which generally focus on specific and more manageable social groups. The resulting projects may not be monumental, but seem to respond better to the needs of particular communities. Because they are smaller, they are also more economically viable and, hence, more likely to get built. What is more, they fit better within the existing fabric of Latin American cities, thereby slowing down their accelerated growth, a situation that is becoming not only uncontrollable but, also, unaffordable. Though large-scale projects continue to be designed, the projects presented in this chapter – and others, such as the hugely successful Favela Barrio Programme in Rio de Janeiro, Brazil[8] – demonstrate that there has been a significant change in the approach to social and low-income housing, a change that has motivated, and continues to generate, interesting and innovative architectural solutions across the continent.

1   See Anderson, B., *Imagined Communities: Reflections on the Origin and Spread of Nationalism.* London/New York: Verso, (1983) 2006.

2   See chapter 'Public Spaces as Contact Zones' for more information on the construction of cable cars in Colombia and Venezuela.

3   In this case, the woven bark panels were replaced by split bamboo branches tied up with vegetable strings.

4   This is important because architectural hybridisation in the Latin American context is often understood as a combination of forms, materials and construction techniques appropriated from Europe and North America with local traditions. As a result, hybridisation is understood as a negative phenomenon, an inferior by-product of the mixture of two (or more) antecedents from Europe or North America which are considered to be 'pure' and hence superior.

5   See 'DissemiNation: Time, Narrative and the Margins of the Modern Nation' in Bhabha, H. K., *The Location of Culture.* London: Routledge, 1994. For a further discussion of the contribution of Bhabha's writing to the development of contemporary architectural theory see Hernández, F., *Bhabha for Architects.* London: Routledge, 2010.

6   See Turner, J. F. C., *Housing by People: Towards Autonomy in Building Environments.* London: Marion Boyars, 1976.

7   As in the case of the projects designed by Affonso Eduardo Reidy (the Pedregulho Housing Complex in Rio de Janeiro, 1950 – 1952) and Carlos Raúl Villanueva (El Paraíso, 1952 – 1954, and Urbanización 23 de Enero, 1955 – 1957).

8   For a further analysis of the Favela Barrio Programme in Rio de Janeiro, see Hernández, F., P. Kellett and L. Allen (eds.) *Rethinking the Informal City: Critical Perspectives from Latin America.* Oxford/New York: Berghahn Books, 2009.

CASA JG, MEDELLÍN, COLOMBIA, CAMILO RESTREPO. VIEW OF THE PASSAGE BETWEEN THE SOCIAL AND ACCOMMODATION BLOCKS.

5 THE PRIVATE HOUSE

Although there is significant variation in the socio-economic and political circumstances of each Latin American country, there is also, in all of them, a dramatic contrast between the conditions of life of the poor majority and those of the wealthy. This is seen in the spatial qualities of buildings and parts of cities which the two groups inhabit, as well as in the modes of property ownership. Indeed, according to statistics, most middle-income/middle-class individuals and families own their house and, often, second holiday homes.[1] Paradoxically, against the realities of poverty brought forward in the previous three chapters, the design of single-family houses and holiday homes is a regular commission for Latin American architects, who, sometimes, amass significant portfolios of this kind of projects while they are still very young. It is precisely because of the youth of their authors that residential architecture often displays great diversity, creativity and vitality, even though the projects are usually small-scale. Rather than underlining similarity throughout the continent, this chapter highlights the diversity that is associated with young architectural practices in Latin America.

In order to challenge the notion of homogeneity often conveyed in publications about Latin American architecture, this chapter includes projects on the coast of the South Atlantic, the Andean lakes, Pampean rivers, the Mexican Pacific coast and, also, a few inner-city houses. This survey does not represent the entirety of architectural production in the continent, nor does it embody generalised architectural tendencies in each individual country. Admittedly, a much larger study would have to be carried out in order to determine with precision the characteristics of contemporary residential architectures in every Latin American country. Therefore, it is necessary to emphasise that one of the aims of this chapter, and of the book in general, is to underline the impossibility of propounding a single identity of Latin American architecture and the need to promulgate the coexistence of multiple architectures – and cultural identities – within the space of each nation without attempting to classify them in any way.

URBAN HOUSES

Casa de la Queja | CALI, COLOMBIA
Benjamin Barney

Queja, which in Spanish means 'complaint', is the name of this house located in San Antonio, a traditional neighbourhood only a few blocks away from the centre of Cali, the third largest

CASA DE LA QUEJA, CALI, COLOMBIA, BENJAMIN BARNEY. VIEW OF THE SOUTHERNMOST COURTYARD AND STAIRWAY TO ROOF-TERRACE.

of Cali allowed Benjamin Barney to create an architecture that does not require mechanical means of ventilation; nor is there the need for illumination during the day.

A minimum number of original rammed-earth walls were kept at the entrance of the house, mainly in order to preserve its exterior image. However, all new walls are made of concrete block. The oversized circular columns around the three court-yards are made of cast-in-situ concrete, as well as the floor slabs which were cast on a wooden deck that forms the ceiling underneath the concrete. The three perpendicular crossings are covered by 45° terracotta-tiled pitched roofs – as is traditional in the region. All structural materials are exposed; nothing is covered by plaster or painting or by any other means. Thus, Barney's house articulates a traditional building typology that was introduced by the Spanish colonisers with contemporary industrial materials put together by artisan builders.

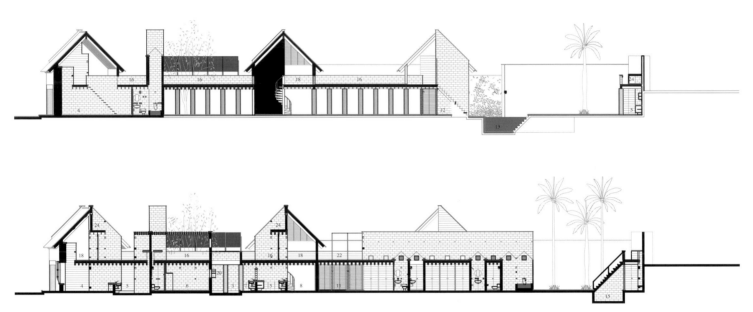

CASA DE LA QUEJA. SECTIONS.

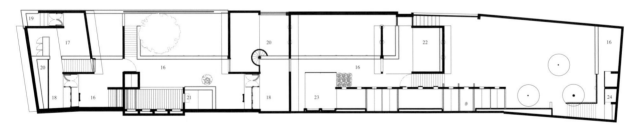

CASA DE LA QUEJA. FIRST FLOOR PLAN.

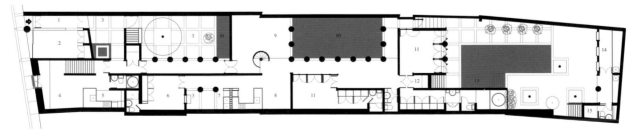

CASA DE LA QUEJA. GROUND FLOOR PLAN.

1 Zaguán
2 Garage
3 Entry courtyard
4 Front apartment
5 Kitchenette
6 Service quarters
7 Launderette
8 Dining room and kitchen
9 Living room
10 Pond
11 Bedroom
12 Storage
13 Swimming pool
14 Changing room
15 Bathroom and swimming pool equipment
16 Open terrace
17 Attic
18 Mezzanine
19 Balcony over entry
20 Void
21 Void over services
22 Upper lounge
23 Hammock
24 Countertop

HOUSE IN RIBEIRÃO PRETO, BRAZIL, ANGELO BUCCI. VIEW OF THE COURTYARD, ACCESS AND THE SOCIAL AREA.

House in Ribeirão Preto | BRAZIL
Angelo Bucci

The house designed by Angelo Bucci and his team Fernando de Mello Franco, Marta Moreira and Milton Braga in Ribeirão Preto in 2001 is another interpretation of the courtyard typology that responds to the urban conditions of contemporary Brazilian suburbia. Ribeirão Preto is a medium-size and relatively affluent city approximately 300 kilometres north-east of São Paulo where temperatures vary between 18°C (winter) and 30°C (summer). Bucci's house in Ribeirão Preto is extroverted and open, rather than unassuming and inward-looking like the previous project. In this case, the house is elevated on columns and, so, it becomes highly visible from the street. Furthermore, the front of the house is fully glazed, which exposes the social areas to the public during the day and, also, at night. The space underneath the house was treated as a landscape where three elevated gardens, each at a different height, demarcate the access and separate functional areas such as

the garage, laundry and general storage. The only habitable volume on ground level is an *en suite* bedroom for employees located at the rear, below the private quarters. Such a configuration transforms the entrance to the house into a journey that requires people to walk under the living and dining room before going upstairs onto one of the elevated gardens in the courtyard from which it is possible to enter the house. Once inside, the hallway offers two options: on the right is the social area (at front) and to the left are the bedrooms (at the back). The kitchen is the connector between the two parts of the house. This way, the amount of circulation space is minimised and the kitchen can be used unobtrusively from either part of the residence. At the back, the bathrooms form a cushion – visual as well as acoustic – between the courtyard and the bedrooms which open onto the rear garden.

Thus, the volume containing the living and dining room is the only fully transparent part of the house. The immense glass panels slide on both sides of the volume permitting not only views through the living room but, also, cross ventilation on hot

HOUSE IN RIBEIRÃO PRETO. VIEW OF THE CAR-PORT AND THE PEDESTRIAN APPROACH TO THE HOUSE UNDER THE SOCIAL AREA. THE ELEVATED COURTYARD CAN BE SEEN IN THE BACKGROUND.

HOUSE IN RIBEIRÃO PRETO. VIEW FROM THE STREET: MAIN ELEVATION.

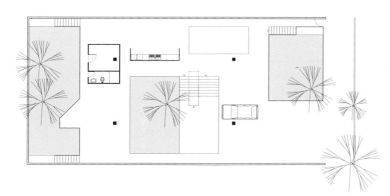

HOUSE IN RIBEIRÃO PRETO. GROUND FLOOR PLAN.

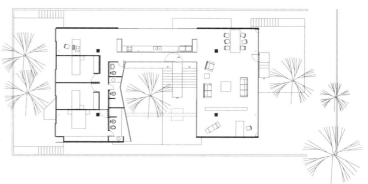

HOUSE IN RIBEIRÃO PRETO. FIRST FLOOR PLAN.

days. However, transparency does not preclude surprise; only by moving through the house can the qualities of its different spaces be experienced fully.

In order to free enough headroom for habitation underneath the house, the slender floor slabs and the roof hang from two deep concrete beams that protrude on top of the house. The concrete is exposed both in and outside the house. Only a few concrete elements are painted, the rest is left bare. The bi-chromatic colour palette facilitates spatial legibility and maximises contrast between the man-made elements and the exuberant vegetation that surrounds the house. It can be argued that some areas are over-exposed to the public and that privacy is sacrificed in order to emphasise the structural audacity. On the other hand, it can also be argued that what is lost in privacy is gained in luminosity and spatial fluidity. Although this house is another reinterpretation of the half-courtyard typology examined in the previous case study, there are significant differences between the two. Not only are such differences seen in the form of both buildings and in the use of certain materials, but, more importantly, in the fact that they represent contrasting conceptualisations of the notion of dwelling. While Barney's house is introverted and focuses on private living, Bucci's house is outward-facing and distinctly exposed; the life of the residents is put on display.

Casa Abu & Font | ASUNCIÓN, PARAGUAY
Gabinete de Arquitectura – Solano Benitez

The practice led by Solano Benitez in Asunción, Paraguay, is concerned with the realities of poverty that affect contemporary architectural practices in his and other Latin American countries. For that reason, they have carried out extensive research on the use of brick – the most inexpensive and common construction material in Paraguay – and their projects explore the structural, aesthetic and socio-economic dimensions of this material. That is why, in their projects, brick is made to work as structure, partition, floor finish and ceiling. Indeed, the work of Solano Benitez is structurally audacious, even though its audacity is not necessarily conspicuous.

The Casa Abu & Font from 2008, for example, could be described as an arch. The party walls contain the structure which supports the first floor slab and the roof. This allows the ground floor to remain a continuous space from the front lawn to the backyard, indeed like an arch that can be closed in the cold days (or whenever necessary) by a series of wood panels that pivot vertically.

The services have been pushed against one of the party walls and are separated from the open living area by a volume

CASA ABU & FONT, ASUNCIÓN, PARAGUAY, GABINETE DE ARQUITECTURA – SOLANO BENITEZ. VIEW OF THE HOUSE FROM THE STREET: MAIN ELEVATION.

which contains two staircases. The width of this volume creates a threshold between the two areas: social and services. An additional ramp on the opposite side of the open living area connects the ground with the first floor, and also helps to conceal the structure. The openness and transparency of the living area removes functional specificity (i.e. there is no dining or living room), turning it into a multi-functional space that can be reinvented by residents according to their needs.

The other two levels of the house, basement and first floor, differ greatly from the ground level and from one another. The basement contains three bedrooms and two bathrooms. It is a cave-like space with no apertures except for a high ribbon window situated below the wooden deck on the backyard. Although it seems inappropriate, these three bedrooms are designed for habitation during winter, when the outside temperatures may drop to -2 °C. Since the soil keeps a stable temperature, which is warmer than the exterior in winter, the basement bedrooms maintain a pleasant temperature without need for artificial heating. The upper level, on the other hand, is significantly larger than the basement, but the layout is extremely convoluted, even labyrinthine. There are four double

CASA ABU & FONT. VIEW OF THE HOUSE FROM THE BACKYARD: BACK ELEVATION.

CASA ABU & FONT. VIEW OF THE MOVABLE WOOD PANELS AT THE REAR OF THE SOCIAL AREA OPENING ONTO TERRACE AND BACKYARD.

bedrooms, two of which are *en suite*. In contrast to the basement, the bedrooms upstairs are long, narrow and have very high ceilings: 5 metres at the uppermost point. Such a configuration generates a constant airflow and helps to preserve cool air inside the bedrooms during the summer months when the temperature may rise to 47°C. Indeed, it could be argued that the convoluted circulation strategy obeys environmental concerns in the sense that it creates air locks which preserve the temperature of the bedrooms. There is also a deliberate attempt to generate thresholds between different parts of the house: from the social to the service area on the ground floor, between floors and, also, between hallway and bedrooms in the

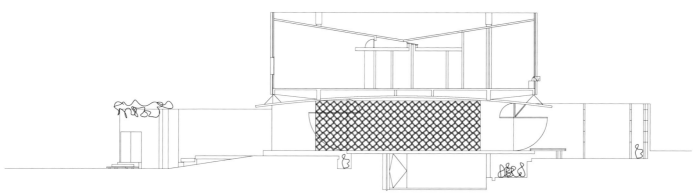

CASA ABU & FONT. LONGITUDINAL SECTION.

CASA ABU & FONT. VIEW OF THE SOCIAL OPEN SPACE ON GROUND LEVEL, STRETCHING FROM THE BACKYARD TO THE FRONT.

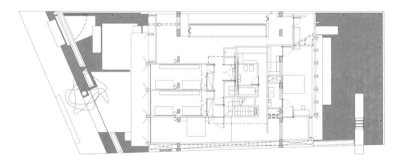

CASA ABU & FONT. FIRST FLOOR PLAN.

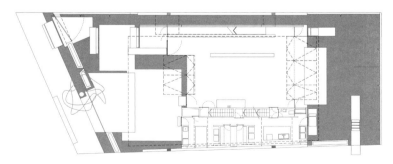

CASA ABU & FONT. GROUND FLOOR PLAN.

CASA ABU & FONT. VIEW OF THE RAMP TO FIRST FLOOR.

upper level. This produces a spatial contrast between public and private areas; the former are ample, luminous and transparent while the latter are intimate, shadowy and secluded.

Existing vegetation was preserved as much as possible and new trees were planted in order to increase protection from the summer heat. The Abu & Font house is an exemplary case of formal, technical and environmental exploration where the patterns of occupation are influenced equally by cultural circumstances as by the particularities of location.

Casa F2 | MEXICO CITY, MEXICO
Isaac Broid, Michael Rojkind and Miguel Adriá

At the opposite end of Latin America, in Mexico, a trio of architects who worked briefly together between 1998 and 2002 designed an award-winning house built in 2002. The house is located in the Condado de Sayavedra, a hilly area with exuberant vegetation on the north-eastern suburbs of Mexico City. The F2 house is conceived as a focus of social activity rather than simply as a residence. Consequently, it was necessary to strike a balance between spaces for public exposure and the intimacy of home. It was also necessary to resolve a significant drop at the back of the site, a topographic condition which presented challenges but, also, provided the opportunity to separate drastically the three zones of the house: 1. recreation on the lower level which serves as bar and playroom but could double as accommodation for guests; 2. social activity and services on the ground level, which contains the access, kitchen and the living and dining rooms; 3. private quarters in the upper level (bedrooms and bathrooms). Each level is orientated differently according to its use. The lower level opens to the garden. The ground level faces south in order to maximise distant views while benefiting from passive solar gain in the winter time. In the upper level, the bedrooms face east so that they look onto the street and receive morning light rather than strong afternoon light.

The structure is a combination of load-bearing walls made of concrete on the outer sides of the L-shape, i.e. the north and west façades of the house. In the inside of the 'L' (east and south façades), a series of metal columns replace the load-bearing walls so that the house opens to the views. This structural configuration conveys a sense of levity, as if the house were floating over the rear garden. This is emphasised by the use of planar concrete elements, both vertically and horizontally, which appear to dematerialise the volumes. Interestingly, this contradicts the natural tectonic of concrete, a material which usually rests heavily on the ground – though it serves the purpose of making the building look light. In this sense,

CASA F2, MEXICO CITY, MEXICO, ISAAC BROID, MICHAEL ROJKIND AND MIGUEL ADRIÁ. VIEW FROM THE BACKYARD.

CASA F2. VIEW OF THE COURTYARD AND THE WESTERN BLOCK FROM THE ACCESS.

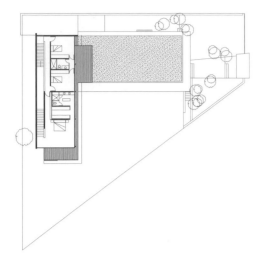

CASA F2. FIRST FLOOR PLAN.

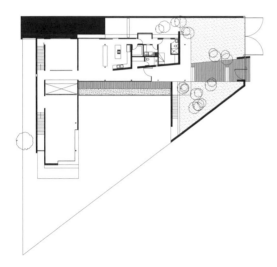

CASA F2. GROUND FLOOR PLAN.

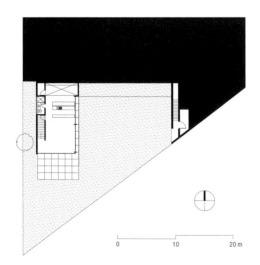

CASA F2. LOWER FLOOR PLAN.

CASA F2. GROUND FLOOR LANDING AND STAIRWELL ON WEST SIDE OF THE HOUSE.

Broid, Rojkind and Adriá depart from the tradition of heavy volumes that was taken to represent Mexican architecture in the work of Barragán, Legorreta and Gonzales de León. What is more, Broid, Rojkind and Adriá rely heavily on factory-made and standardised building components, as well as on industrial construction techniques, rather than hand-made elements and artisan labour.

COASTAL HOUSES

Casa Techos | LAGO NAHUEL HUAPUI, ARGENTINA
Mathias Klotz

Although Mathias Klotz has designed buildings for a variety of functions – including educational, commercial and office uses – his practice is internationally recognised for having amassed a vast portfolio of residential buildings. The Casa Techos from 2006, located in the beautiful lake region of Bariloche, northern Patagonia, is part of this portfolio. Although Bariloche is a remote region, its topographic and climatic conditions make it attractive for tourism throughout the year. During the winter

CASA TECHOS, LAGO NAHUEL HUAPUI, ARGENTINA, MATHIAS KLOTZ. SOUTH ELEVATION.

months it is a popular ski resort while, in the summer time, it is a fashionable destination for trekkers and water sports lovers (although the average temperature of the water is 7°C). Since the area was developing rapidly, the regional government imposed strict building regulations to prevent excessive construction of holiday homes and to maintain a certain visual homogeneity in the town and its surrounding areas. These require all new constructions to have inclined roofs at a minimum gradient of 26° in order to allow the access of natural light. This regulation presented Klotz with a challenge considering that

CASA TECHOS. WEST ELEVATION.

CASA TECHOS. VIEW OF THE SWIMMING POOL AT LOWER LEVEL.

CASA TECHOS. VIEW OF THE INTERIOR FROM THE ENTRYWAY.

CASA TECHOS. VIEW OF THE SOCIAL AREA, CORRIDOR AND STAIRWAY.

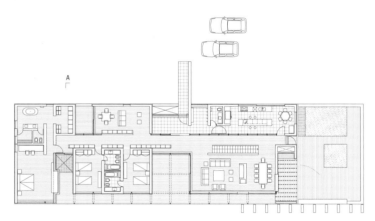

CASA TECHOS. UPPER LEVEL PLAN.

0   5   10 m

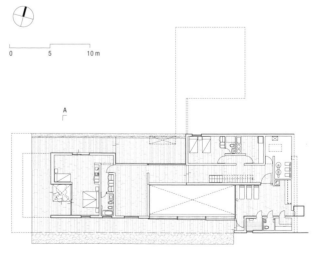

CASA TECHOS. LOWER LEVEL PLAN.

most of his buildings have flat roofs. In addition, it is also specified that new constructions must have views of the lake and the forest. As a response to the regulations, Klotz designed a series of small roofs rather than a double pitch. The multiple roofs permit greater access of natural light from the north (as this is the southern hemisphere), while the house opens towards the lake on the south side. The construction of the multiple roofs required an intricate metal structure which remains exposed in the interior of the house.

The programme was divided in two levels: the upper level contains all the living areas and accommodation while the lower level contains the services and the swimming pool. Simultaneously, each level was divided in two halves. The eastern part

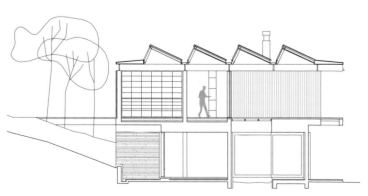

CASA TECHOS. CROSS SECTION A-A.

CASA LA ROCA, PUNTA DEL ESTE, URUGUAY, MATHIAS KLOTZ. EAST ELEVATION.

of the upper level is social and includes the kitchen. The west side of this level contains the bedrooms and a small family room separate from the main social area. A similar distribution is repeated in the lower level where the swimming pool and gymnasium lie on the east, below the social area, and the guest bedroom is on the west, below the living quarters. Considering the sheer size of the house and the programmatic complexity of a luxury holiday home, Klotz was able to create a sense of intimacy and homeliness while, also, pursuing his own personal architectural agenda.

Casa La Roca | PUNTA DEL ESTE, URUGUAY
Mathias Klotz

The Casa La Roca from 2006 is another luxury holiday house designed by Klotz in Uruguay (neither of these two projects is situated in his native Chile). Rather than a quaint Andean lake, this house is located in José Ignacio, a small fishermen's town turned opulent resort, on the shore of the Atlantic Ocean 40 kilometres north-east of Punta del Este, Uruguay. Most new houses built in this rapidly growing popular holiday destination are for temporary occupation during the summer season – December and January – rather than for permanent occupation. The Roca house sits on a rectangular 800-square-metre site, perpendicular to the ocean, on the southernmost tip of José Ignacio. The house consists of two volumes of similar dimensions connected by a bridge on the east side. Together, these three components form an open courtyard. Since the site

slopes down toward the beach and sideways to the east, only the northern volume rests directly on the ground. This three-storey volume contains accommodation for the housekeeper, two double bedrooms and one bathroom on the ground level and the *en suite* master bedroom on the first floor. The single-storey southern volume stands on stilts above the rocks and the beach. It contains the kitchen, living and dining areas, as well as a social bathroom. The space underneath the southern volume is the main entryway and works also as a transition between the

CASA LA ROCA. VIEW FROM THE ROCKS: SOUTH ELEVATION.

CASA EN LA BARANCA, ARROYO SECO, SANTA FE, ARGENTINA, RAFAEL IGLESIA. VIEW OF THE HOUSE FROM THE RIVER.

CASA EN LA BARANCA. VIEW OF THE RIVER FROM THE LEVEL OF THE ENTRANCE TO THE HOUSE.

by load-bearing brick walls. The walls are white-washed, both in and outside, while concrete elements are exposed in most areas of the interior. Though the palette is exceedingly simple, materials are exquisitely articulated in such a way that they create a sense of homeliness and elegance rather than auster-ity. Even though the houses are modest in scale, they have an outstanding spatiality and demonstrate Campodonico's thorough understanding of the conditions of the site. Not only was Campodonico able to satisfy the programme, he was also able to conduct a formal, spatial and environmental experiment while exploiting the extraordinary natural characteristics of the Uruguayan coast.

Casa en La Barranca | ARROYO SECO, SANTA FE, ARGENTINA
Rafael Iglesia

Like the Andean lakes and the oceans, rivers are important elements in the Latin American landscape. In fact, rivers have an immense historical value and play a central role in the economies of many regions throughout the continent. Not surprisingly, Rafael Iglesia is at odds to make the River Paraná both the theme and the focus of this small house built in 1999 and located approximately 30 kilometres south-east of Rosario, the third largest city of Argentina.

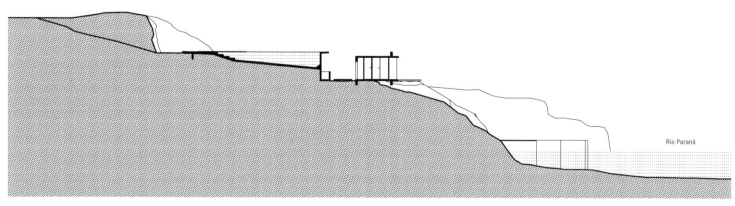

Rio Paraná

CASA EN LA BARANCA. SECTION THROUGH SITE.

CASA EN LA BARANCA. VIEW OF THE SWIMMING POOL AND THE RIVER PARANÁ.

CASA EN LA BARANCA. VIEW OF THE SWIMMING POOL GIVING THE IMPRESSION THAT IT IS AN EXTENSION OF THE RIVER PARANÁ.

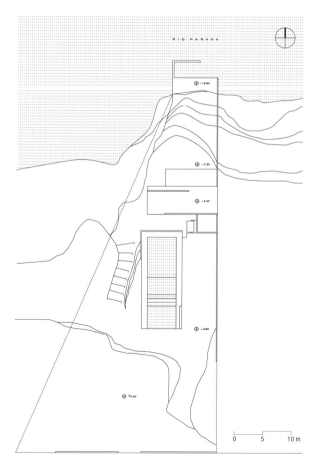

CASA EN LA BARANCA. SITE PLAN.

The project is conceived as a journey from the street to the water passing through four different levels or plateaus. At street level, the first plateau is an open lawn from which only the river and the immense Pampa can be seen on the horizon. The second plateau, containing nothing else but a swimming pool, emerges as one progresses into the site. The swimming pool area is secluded from the street and opens towards the river which can be seen beyond the roof of the house (now visible). A steep walkway on the eastern side of the swimming pool leads down to the third plateau, where one finally meets the house. The house is a single rectangular space with a kitchen and a bathroom. The north façade is a continuous span of glass only interrupted by a wall necessary to support the roof. The living room opens onto a generous wooden deck which gives the impression of floating over the river. The journey continues down towards a small jetty which works as the final link in the succession of spaces connecting the street above with the river below.

Indeed, the project is exceedingly simple and relies greatly on theatricality as a source of drama. The roughness of the materials, the water cascading on one side of the swimming pool, the terrace cantilevering over the river, all these features disclose an interesting plasticity and create a strong conceptual link with the site. On the other hand, the enormous north-facing glass span, which receives direct sunlight all day, raises

CASA EN LA BARANCA. VIEW OF THE ACCESS TO THE HOUSE WITH WATER CASCADING FROM THE SWIMMING POOL.

Observatory House | ESTADO DE OAXACA, MEXICO
Tatiana Bilbao

On the Pacific Coast of Mexico, at the other extreme of Latin America, architect Tatiana Bilbao collaborated with artist Gabriel Orozco in 2006 to build a retreat house on the beach. The project is almost a complete replica of the Jantar Mantar astronomical observatory built in Delhi at the beginning of the 18th century. Indeed, on a superficial level, the idea of an observatory fits the purpose of the retreat house that Bilbao designed with and for Orozco: a house which is, also, a platform to 'observe' the sea, the coast line, the country landscape and, of course, the sky. The implications of such a translation, however, are more complex. Bilbao argues that such a cultural, historical and geographical displacement is related to the artist's tradition of linking and mixing unusual and often forgotten elements – both in his art and architectural projects. Orozco does that mixing in order to provoke unexpected socio-political responses from his audience. Thus, the architect adds, the house is a creative instrument for the artist. Bilbao's interesting argument appears to be somewhat unsuitable, however, because a private house differs greatly from an art form which comes into direct contact with the public at exhibitions, where people can respond to it. So, while the house may be a creative instrument for the architect, it could hardly provoke collective socio-political responses from the public.

An important question arises here regarding the architectural implications of appropriating forms and images from other cultures. Needless to say, this is an important and unresolved debate in the context of contemporary architecture in Latin America. To be sure, the entire history of Latin American architecture has been written in 'comparative mode' or, as explained

questions about heat in a region where temperatures could rise above 30°C in the summer and rarely fall below 9°C in the winter. Nevertheless, this house is the result of an interesting formal and material exploration and, for that reason, it was shortlisted for the second Mies van der Rohe Award along with Benjamin Barney's Casa de la Queja.

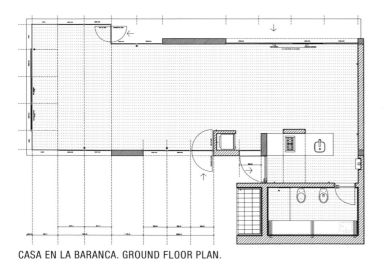

CASA EN LA BARANCA. GROUND FLOOR PLAN.

OBSERVATORY HOUSE, ESTADO DE OAXACA, MEXICO, TATIANA BILBAO. GENERAL VIEW OF THE HOUSE.

OBSERVATORY HOUSE. SIDE ELEVATION.

OBSERVATORY HOUSE. VIEW OF THE HOUSE WITH PACIFIC OCEAN IN THE BACKGROUND.

in the introduction, in relation to European (and North American) referents which set the rule against which all architectural production is continually judged – in Latin America as well as in other peripheries. This method of architectural historicisation presents non-western architectures always as transformations of European and North American forms, techniques and ideas, indistinctively of whether they are openly discriminated (i.e. considered to be deviations and devaluations of a cosmopolitan original) or ratified as ingenious adaptations of either classic or modern architectures to the particularities of the periphery. This debate is broader and more complex than can be addressed in this brief study of a house by an individual Mexican artist. Nev-

ertheless, there is an issue which deserves some attention: the fact that Bilbao and Orozco are appropriating from Indian architecture rather than from Europe and North America. This issue is particularly important because it reveals a new dynamics of cultural interaction between previously colonised countries – or so-called peripheries – which, to some extent, bypasses the control of empire. In other words, it appears that the transfer of architectural discourses (and forms) is no longer monopolised by the west (Europe and North America). Previously colonised countries and other peripheries have established channels of transcultural communication outside the axiality of binary divisions between east and west (or colonised and coloniser,

OBSERVATORY HOUSE. VIEW OF THE TERRACES AND STAIRS FORMING AN INTRICATE CONTINUOUS OUTDOOR CIRCULATION SYSTEM.

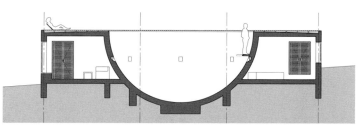

OBSERVATORY HOUSE. CROSS SECTION.

CASA DE CAMPO EN LA PLAYOSA. VIEW OF THE FORECOURT DEMARCATING THE APPROACH TO THE HOUSE.

CASA DE CAMPO EN LA PLAYOSA. VIEW OF THE FORECOURT AND ACCESS.

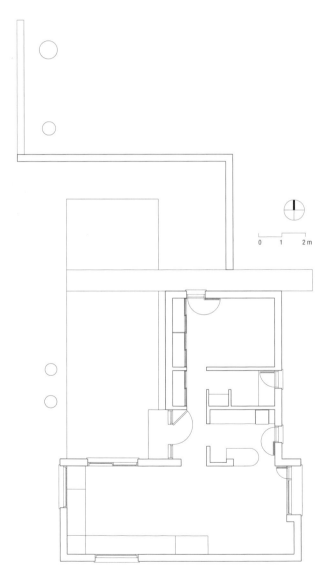

CASA DE CAMPO EN LA PLAYOSA. GROUND FLOOR PLAN.

articulated. Another aspect that deserves mentioning is the way in which the architect tackles harsh environmental conditions and creates a homely environment with minimum resources in a desolate site.

Casa JG | MEDELLÍN, COLOMBIA
Camilo Restrepo

Camilo Restrepo is amongst those architects who have amassed a large portfolio of residential architecture while still being very young. Most of his work is located in Medellín, the second largest city of Colombia. Restrepo finds inspiration in the mountainous topography and takes advantage of the favourable climatic conditions of the region. The Casa JG, for example, was built in 2007 in a subdivision on the south-eastern hills of the city, a few kilometres outside the metropolitan

CASA JG, MEDELLÍN, COLOMBIA, CAMILO RESTREPO. VIEW OF THE HOUSE FROM THE NORTH-WEST WITH FRONT TERRACE, SOCIAL AREA AND VOLUME OF ACCOMMODATION ON THE RIGHT.

CASA JG. NIGHT VIEW OF THE HOUSE FROM THE SOUTH-EAST.

area. The sloping terrain offers wonderful views of the city but, at the same time, leaves the house exposed to other dwellings which sit on higher ground at the rear. Such a situation determined the general layout of the house which uses the services and circulation spaces as visual barriers on the east side. That way, the living and dining rooms, as well as bedrooms, can enjoy unobstructed views of the city and the western hills on the opposite side of the Aburrá Valley.

The three main bodies of the house are separated by irregular recesses that form narrow internal passages into one another and playful nooks outside. The northernmost block contains the garage, laundry and the maid's apartment. The central block houses the kitchen and the social area (dining and living room). Although the main entrance appears to be prominent in the plan, its location at the back of the house, makes it imperceptible at first glance and, hence, spatially inconsequent.

CASA JG. SOUTH ELEVATION.

CASA JG. LOWER LEVEL PLAN.

The southernmost block of the house contains the bedrooms which are distributed in two levels: the upper level is occupied entirely by the master bedroom while the lower level is dedicated to the children. It comprises two ample bedrooms and a nursery/playroom, which can later be transformed into a study room.

As if replicating the rugged topographic contours, the roof appears as a disjointed series of protruding volumes. In fact, these are lightwells that reach out for natural light to illuminate areas of the house which would otherwise be dark (hallways, bathrooms and wardrobes). Although inaccessible, the roof can

be considered as a topography in its own right which establishes a formal connection with the natural surroundings. Like other houses designed by Restrepo, the JG house demonstrates the architect's interest in carrying out formal, spatial and material explorations inspired by the natural conditions of the region.

The eleven houses examined in this chapter show the great variety of residential work currently being produced by architects in Latin America. As mentioned at the beginning, this survey cannot be taken to represent architectural tendencies in a generalised manner. Instead, the purpose of this chapter

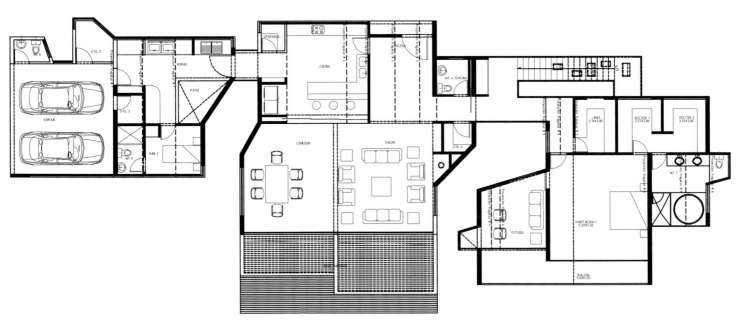

CASA JG. GROUND FLOOR PLAN.

CASA JG. DETAIL OF THE BACK ELEVATION (EAST) SHOWING THE STAIRCASE TO THE CHILDREN'S QUARTERS.

is to prove that more thorough studies of recent architectural production are necessary in order to develop theories capable of dealing with such heterogeneity and with the speed at which newer approaches continue to appear.

It is important to stress that the architects whose work is included in this chapter have large portfolios and, in many cases, different buildings show different formal characteristics. Architects like Tatiana Bilbao, Camilo Restrepo and Michael Rojkind, for example, employ comfortably different methods of design depending on the circumstances of each project. This ability to adapt and recast their practices regularly has been examined by critics in other fields, particularly in the visual arts, but not in architecture. For example Néstor García Canclini explores a similar phenomenon in the work of borderline Mexican artists.[3] Canclini explains that many contemporary artists, especially those of indigenous origin, move swiftly across language barriers (they speak fluent Spanish and English as well as their own indigenous languages). Also, in their artwork, these artists articulate elements from their own cultural traditions with aspects of modern European and North American art. They perform these complex operations in order to penetrate the international art market. Canclini describes this cultural phenomenon as cultural hybridity. It is important to note, however, that hybridity is not found *only* in the artwork itself (which mixes bits from various origins) but also, and more importantly, in the cultural milieu where the artwork emerges. In other words, it is not just the artwork (the painting, sculpture, installation or video), it is the culture which is hybrid. That is why the notion of hybridity appears to be suitable in order to examine the strategies used by many contemporary architects in Latin America to both get their work built and to penetrate international networks of architectural dissemination. Almost all architects in this chapter have successfully penetrated the increasingly globalised architectural market: they build in various countries, teach at universities in Europe and North America and exhibit internationally. They have done so by transgressing cultural

CASA JG. VIEW OF THE PASSAGE BETWEEN THE SOCIAL AND PRIVATE BLOCKS.

CASA JG. VIEW OF MEDELLÍN FROM THE SOCIAL AREA.

CASA JG. WESTERN TERRACE, OUTSIDE THE SOCIAL AREA.

barriers and by constantly articulating a wide range of architectural discourses, formal languages and construction techniques. For that reason, their work cannot be easily classified as part of any national or continental identity. Nevertheless, aspects such as their nationality and professional registration, for example, inevitably reconstruct their national affiliations. Indeed, this contradiction lies at the centre of discussions about cultural hybridity which focus on the gaps that open between cultures and cultural practices (i.e. art, architecture, literature, language and, also, less tangible forms such as patterns of consumption). In other words, it is in the *inter*-national space (between nations and national affiliations) where hybridisation occurs.

ARTIST'S STUDIO. VIEW OF THE FORECOURT AND ACCESS FROM THE INTERIOR: THE RAMP FOR VEHICLES IS ON THE LEFT AND THE PEDESTRIAN ACCESS IS ON THE RIGHT.

ARTIST'S STUDIO, MEXICO CITY, MEXICO, TATIANA BILBAO. VIEW OF THE FORECOURT AND CANTILEVER FROM THE PEDESTRIAN ACCESS TO THE PROPERTY.

ARTIST'S STUDIO. VIEW OF THE MAIN GALLERY SPACE.

ARCHITECTURAL AND CULTURAL HYBRIDITY

Artist's Studio | MEXICO CITY, MEXICO
Tatiana Bilbao

Let us pause here for a moment in order to examine briefly the argument about cultural hybridity in the work of Tatiana Bilbao and Michael Rojkind by way of two examples (the Orquideorama, included in the next chapter, demonstrates Camilo Restrepo's ability to do the same). The first is a studio for another artist designed by Bilbao[4] in Mexico City between 2007 and 2008. Unlike the coastal retreat for Orozco which is a relatively simple building, the programme for the building in Mexico City requires a large studio and exhibition space as

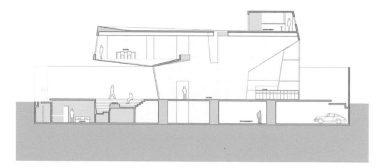

ARTIST'S STUDIO. LONGITUDINAL SECTION.

ARTIST'S STUDIO. DETAIL OF THE STAIRCASE.

ARTIST'S STUDIO. VIEW OF THE MAIN GALLERY FROM MEZZANINE LEVEL.

well as offices and housing for an artist in residence, kitchen, services, a multi-functional area for social events (such as exhibition openings) and parking for 25 cars. This time, Bilbao opted for angular shapes, large cantilevers and big windows that allow plenty of natural light into the studio as well as into most parts of the building. The levity conveyed by the cantilever is reinforced by the whiteness of all the surfaces (walls, floors and ceilings), which also introduces a sense of cleanliness and 'cosmopolitan' sophistication. Indeed, the projects designed by Bilbao demonstrate her ability continually to re-cast herself as a designer and articulate elements taken from different sources (cultural, historical and architectural) in the production of buildings which do not, necessarily, correspond with any prescribed idea of Mexicaness.

Nestlé Chocolate Museum | TOLUCA, MEXICO
Michael Rojkind

Similarly, in recent projects Michael Rojkind has moved away from the 'exploded box' approach seen in the F2 house that he designed with Isaac Broid and Miguel Adriá. As an independent practitioner, Rojkind has shown a predilection for angular forms made of metal and for the use of bright colours as a way to stand out rather than blend with the context.

His Nestlé Chocolate Museum in Toluca, Mexico, from 2007 is a clear example. The building is conceived as an elongated hetero-morphous volume elevated on *pilotis*. The museum has a corporate façade towards the car park and the motorway but appears to be more informal on all its other sides. The bright red colour of the exterior contrasts dramatically with the pristine white of all interior surfaces (floors, walls and ceilings); only a green carpet in the main media room interrupts the otherwise all-white interior. In general, the Nestlé Chocolate Museum subscribes to a completely different architectural narrative than his earlier work. Indeed, Rojkind's work continues to change every time he takes on newer challenges. The point to make is that the vitality of this search for architectural identity cannot be discussed in terms of nationality (or national identity), nor can it be entirely attributed to a desire to be part of specific movements (such as modernism, for example) – which is different from saying that contemporary architects like Bilbao and Rojkind are not interested in receiving national and international recognition. Identity, for this younger generation of architects, is a dynamic, somewhat imprecise construct formed in the interstices between cultures, nations, practices and so on.

Under these circumstances, hybridisation ceases to be a negative occurrence – as has often been understood in archi-

NESTLÉ CHOCOLATE MUSEUM, TOLUCO, MEXICO, MICHAEL ROJKIND. MAIN ACCESS.

NESTLÉ CHOCOLATE MUSEUM. VIEW OF THE POLYMORPHOUS VOLUME.

NESTLÉ CHOCOLATE MUSEUM. MAIN MEDIA ROOM.

NESTLÉ CHOCOLATE MUSEUM. VIEW OF THE PUBLIC FAÇADE.

NESTLÉ CHOCOLATE MUSEUM. INTERIOR CIRCULATION.

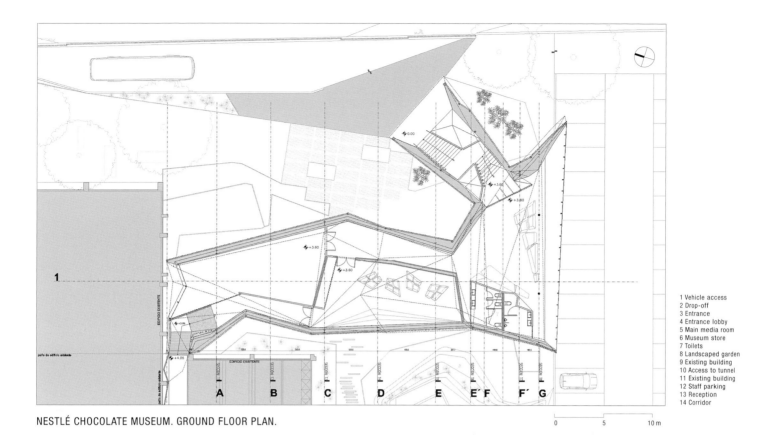

1 Vehicle access
2 Drop-off
3 Entrance
4 Entrance lobby
5 Main media room
6 Museum store
7 Toilets
8 Landscaped garden
9 Existing building
10 Access to tunnel
11 Existing building
12 Staff parking
13 Reception
14 Corridor

NESTLÉ CHOCOLATE MUSEUM. GROUND FLOOR PLAN.

0   5   10 m

tectural discourse – and becomes a sign of cultural productivity, a sign of the creativity and ingenuity of architects across Latin America. By understanding contemporary architectural practices in Latin America as the result of continuous processes of internal and external hybridisation (that is, inside each country, as in the case of Alexia León's Teatina-Quincha Shelter, and between the countries of Latin America and others outside, as in the case of Bilbao and Rojkind), it is possible to disturb the bipolarity of existing methods of critique according to which they are a derivation of the Euro-American canon (as explained in the introduction). It is not that existing architectural hierarchies are dismantled completely, or that Europe and North America lose their authority altogether. However, the recognition of authority

becomes difficult due to the proliferation of difference that these practices exemplify. That is why I have affirmed that the notion of cultural hybridisation brings forward the productivity of cultural and architectural difference rather than striving for its elimination. I have insisted on the existence of difference in this and previous chapters because an outstanding characteristic of contemporary Latin America is that the differences between nations, peoples and cultures are more clearly perceived and strongly enacted now than they have ever been before. For that reason, I have also insisted on the importance of not seeing Latin American architecture as an undifferentiated totality but, on the contrary, as a dynamic, complex and multifaceted field that escapes straightforward classification.

1 According to statistics provided by the governments of Argentina, Chile, Colombia, Mexico and Uruguay, an average 75 percent of middle- and high-income individuals and families own their residential property. Similarly, an average 35 percent (across the countries listed above) of middle- and high-income families own a holiday home outside the city.

2 Luís Barragán, Rogelio Salmona and Eladio Dieste, for example, never built in countries different from their own. Oscar Niemeyer, on the other hand, produced buildings in many countries including Israel, USA and, more recently, the United Kingdom.

3 See García Canclini, N., *Culturas Híbridas: Estrategias para Entrar y Salir de la Modernidad*. Mexico: Editorial Paidós, 2002 (reprint). – English edition:

Hybrid Cultures. Strategies for Entering and Leaving Modernity. Minneapolis: University of Minnesota Press, 1995.

4 In collaboration with Francisco Pardo, Julio Amezcua, Israel Álvarez, Aida Hurtado, Arturo Peniche, Jorge Vázquez, Carlos Leguizamo and Octavio Vázquez who also contributed to the Observatory House.

ORQUIDEORAMA, MEDELLÍN, COLOMBIA, PLAN B ARQUITECTOS AND JPRCR ARQUITECTOS.

6 ARCHITECTURE IN THE LANDSCAPE

After having analysed buildings and public spaces embedded in the fabric of Latin American cities, and reviewing the imaginative ways in which architects tackle poverty and overcrowding, as well as opulence, I would like to focus on the relationship between buildings and their natural surroundings in various parts of the continent. The previous chapter already underlined the diversity of environments that exist in such a vast and geographically imprecise region that is Latin America. It included houses on the Pacific and the Atlantic Oceans, on the banks of rivers and the edges of lakes, in cities as well as in the country. This chapter reinforces the notion of environmental diversity but focuses particularly on the way in which architects respond to the challenges presented by such a diverse landscapes. It reveals the strategies employed by architects to juggle environmental concerns with their own architectural agendas, and the way in which they engage with issues relating to history, technology, economics and social politics.

HOTEL EXPLORA, SAN PEDRO DE ATACAMA, CHILE, GERMÁN DEL SOL. VIEW OF THE RAMP LEADING TO THE BAR AND RESTAURANT.

It becomes apparent that geographical and cultural differences preclude the implementation of generalised solutions or design formulas that can be applied everywhere. Design strategies need to be revised, and often rethought entirely, from one project to another. Not only can this be seen in the analysis of buildings designed by different architects in diverse countries but, also, in the work of individual architects whose buildings differ greatly from one another. In this sense, I will develop further another aspect that was introduced in the previous section, namely the capacity of contemporary architects to adapt their practices and, so, their own identities, to continually shifting circumstances.

The analysis of these projects puts forward a sophisticated understanding of the landscape or, else, the natural context. The samples analysed in this chapter demonstrate that, more than a set of physical characteristics, the landscape includes people, their histories and cultures, and, in many cases, the traumas left by decades of economic (and political) abandonment. That is the case for communities in the Atacama Desert

and Isla de Pascua, two regions which endured the brutality of Spanish colonisation and latter suffered again from the decline of their industries – nitrate mining and sheep farming respectively. Socio-political awareness on the part of the architects makes each project unique but, at the same time, brings forward a number of inherent contradictions. Admittedly, the intricacy of the historical and cultural issues I am referring to cannot be resolved merely by the construction of buildings. What is more, this chapter points out that, in many cases, buildings may contribute to accentuate clashes between cultural or socio-economic groups. The three first cases, for example, are stylish – and, so, relatively expensive – hotels which bring benefits to local residents but, simultaneously, exacerbate cultural and socio-economic difference by various means. Not only do they bring a wealthy class of 'world travellers' to the places where they are built, but their mere presence near small towns and communities causes a politico-economic re-classification of the land which, in turn, rules out poor residents from the area. The architects are clearly aware of the effects that their buildings

HOTEL EXPLORA. PRELIMINARY SKETCHES BY THE ARCHITECT.

HOTEL EXPLORA, ISLA DE PASCUA, CHILE, JOSÉ CRUZ OVALLE. INTERSEC-
TION BETWEEN VARIOUS VOLUMES. THE DIFFERENT LEVELS ARE ARTICULATED
VERTICALLY THROUGH RAMPS AND STAIRWAYS.

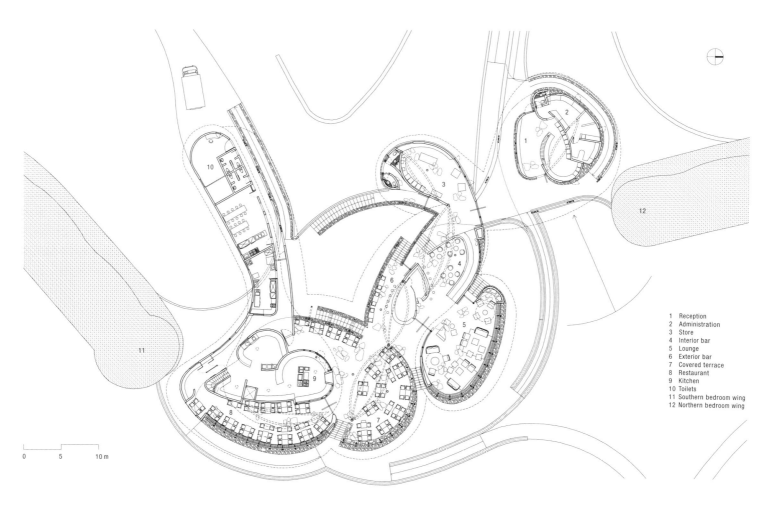

1 Reception
2 Administration
3 Store
4 Interior bar
5 Lounge
6 Exterior bar
7 Covered terrace
8 Restaurant
9 Kitchen
10 Toilets
11 Southern bedroom wing
12 Northern bedroom wing

HOTEL EXPLORA. GROUND FLOOR PLAN.

HOTEL EXPLORA. VIEW OF THE PERIPHERAL CIRCULATIONS UNDER THE CANOPY AND THE ARTICULATION OF MATERIALS ON THE EXTERIOR OF THE BUILDING.

HOTEL EXPLORA. VIEW OF THE INTERIOR OF THE HOTEL AND THE ARTICULATION OF MATERIALS IN THE LOBBY.

devised by Latin American architects in response to the natural and socio-political circumstances of each place.

In order to describe Isla de Pascua, for example, Cruz explains the undulating horizontality of the site – horizontality both in geometrical terms as well as in its relation to the horizon – which is perceived in the form of three lines that separate the land from the sky, the land from the ocean and the ocean from the sky. Such distant intangible lines are the only spatial demarcation in the vastness of the Pacific Ocean. The position of the eye in the vertical axis determines the predominance of one of these three lines and, accordingly, the relationship one establishes with the horizon.

Cruz also studied the *moais* (also spelt *mohais*), the distinctive *Rapa Nui* statues found in the island, which generally stand on a stone platform, or *ahu*. Rather than setting a limit to the island's space, Cruz argues that they frame the view of the horizon. In other words, for Cruz, the void between the figures is as important as the figures themselves. He also notes that

neither positive nor negative space is rectilinear – everything you can see is curved.

These two analyses influenced the form of the Hotel Explora from 2005, which is conceived as a series of separate curved volumes elevated on a platform. The volumes modify the way the landscape is perceived. Just like the *moais* standing on the *ahus*, the volumes generate a multitude of spaces around and inside the hotel. Such spaces are connected by an intricate circulation system that includes ramps, stairwells and weaving corridors. The complex circulation system repositions the viewer constantly at different heights so that his or her relationship with the horizon is never the same.

Although the plan suggests great spatial complexity, the layout is very simple. There is a main volume in the centre which contains the services and all public areas (lobby, restaurant, bar, kitchen, etc.). Two wings of the bedrooms extend towards the north and the south-west adapting to the contour lines. Access is gained through a ramp that connects the car park in the

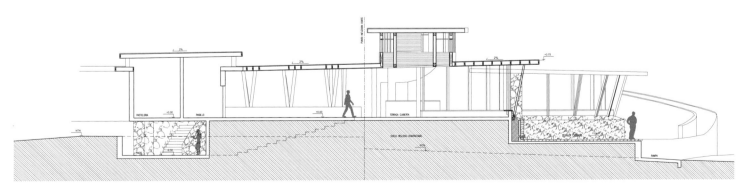

HOTEL EXPLORA. CROSS SECTION.

north-west with the reception in the central volume. Internal circulations are placed on the north and north-west side in such a way that all inhabitable areas open towards the ocean which is approximately 2 kilometres away from the hotel in the south and south-east direction.

The rustic, yet elegant exterior makes a stark contrast with the interior where concrete floors are polished and the wood-work that characterises Cruz's oeuvre is impeccable.[4] Thus, the interior is both stylish and warm at the same time – a sense of homeliness which, as in the previous two projects, results from the articulation of seemingly opposing materials.

Postgraduate Building, Universidad Adolfo Ibañez |
SANTIAGO DE CHILE, CHILE
José Cruz Ovalle

Back in the capital Santiago, where he has his studio, Cruz was commissioned to design a postgraduate educational facility for the Universidad Adolfo Ibañez. He had already designed the undergraduate building for the same institution, a project that he completed in 2002 and for which he received the First Prize at the Bienal Iberoamericana de Arquitectura y Urbanismo (Lima, Peru, 2004). The new facility was to be located on a site nearby. In his description of the project, Cruz demonstrates a great deal of self-criticism by indicating that there were excesses in

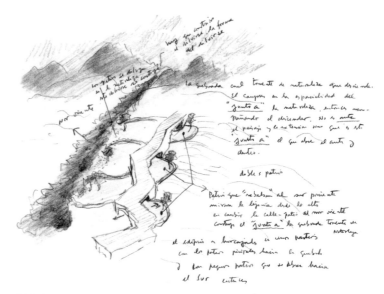

POSTGRADUATE BUILDING, UNIVERSIDAD ADOLFO IBAÑEZ, SANTIAGO DE CHILE, CHILE, JOSÉ CRUZ OVALLE, PRELIMINARY SKETCHES BY THE ARCHITECT.

his design for the undergraduate building, excesses which he did not want to repeat in the centre for postgraduate studies. Though there are some similarities between the two schemes, it is safe to affirm that the latter building, completed in 2007, shows a greater level of accomplishment. Not only is this judgement based on the usage of a more complex morphology but,

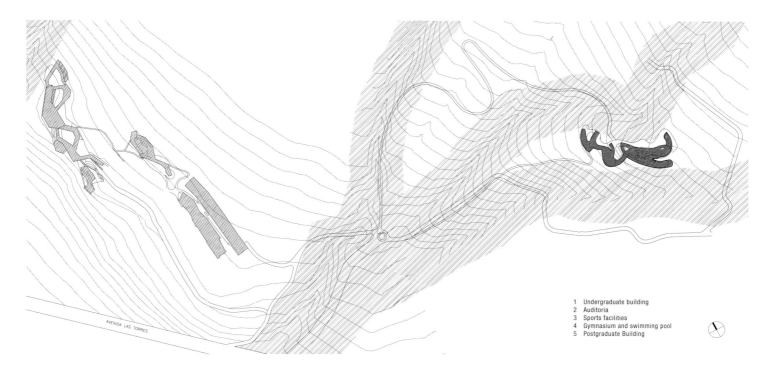

1 Undergraduate building
2 Auditoria
3 Sports facilities
4 Gymnasium and swimming pool
5 Postgraduate Building

POSTGRADUATE BUILDING, UNIVERSIDAD ADOLFO IBAÑEZ. SITE PLAN SHOWING THE TWO BUILDINGS BY JOSÉ CRUZ OVALLE: THE UNDERGRADUATE BUILDING (LEFT) AND THE POSTGRADUATE COMPLEX (RIGHT).

POSTGRADUATE BUILDING, UNIVERSIDAD ADOLFO IBAÑEZ. AERIAL VIEW OF THE BUILDING SHOWING ITS CORRESPONDENCE TO THE MORPHOLOGY OF THE *CORDILLERA*.

POSTGRADUATE BUILDING, UNIVERSIDAD ADOLFO IBAÑEZ. VIEW OF THE BUILDING FROM THE ROAD ILLUSTRATING ITS RELATION WITH THE LANDSCAPE.

POSTGRADUATE BUILDING, UNIVERSIDAD ADOLFO IBAÑEZ. VIEW OF THE UNDULATING VOLUMES AND THE EXTERIOR CIRCULATIONS.

POSTGRADUATE BUILDING, UNIVERSIDAD ADOLFO IBAÑEZ. VIEW OF THE PUBLIC AREAS ON THE NORTH-EASTERN SIDE OF THE BUILDING.

also, on the creation of a dynamic and extraordinarily diverse spatiality.

The site consisted of a steep and narrow ridge extending out of the *cordillera* towards the city. Although it is not the most appropriate location from an economic and, even, technical point of view (because of the cost and difficulty of building on a rugged and steep terrain), Cruz placed the building on top of the ridge. Two reasons motivated this decision: first, it

guarantees views of the city in front and the Andes at the back, second, that way the building is distanced 250 metres from the main road. This distance constitutes a transition into the building, a gradual detachment from the city (first by car, then on foot) and a reduction of speed, so that arrival into the place of study happens at the slower pace of the pedestrian.

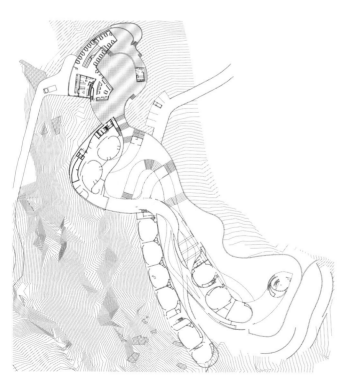

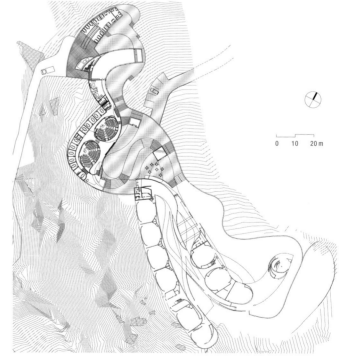

POSTGRADUATE BUILDING, UNIVERSIDAD ADOLFO IBAÑEZ. LOWER LEVEL PLAN.

POSTGRADUATE BUILDING, UNIVERSIDAD ADOLFO IBAÑEZ. INTERMEDIATE LEVEL PLAN.

POSTGRADUATE BUILDING, UNIVERSIDAD ADOLFO IBAÑEZ. VIEW OF THE INTERIOR AND THE AERIAL CIRCULATION SYSTEM COMPOSED OF RAMPS AND BRIDGES.

The building or, indeed, buildings – for it consists of an arrangement of intertwined volumes – create a series of outdoor public spaces (patios) on different levels at the north-east where they receive the morning sunlight. A few interruptions in the continuity of the weaving building at ground level permit controlled views of the city from the patios. However, other volumes float above these intermittent interruptions creating covered plazas, protected from the sunlight, where students can gather in the afternoon. The undulations of the buildings are not arbitrary. As the architect explains, they make room for different natural occurrences: a tree here, a rock there or a needed transparency over there. Those particularities of the site – which are not common to any other site – determine the form of the building, its position on the site and the undulations of the volumes. Similar considerations were made for the location of windows, ramps, stairwells and all major components of the postgraduate complex. What can be perceived as arbitrary in photos of the exterior of the building, or in plans, is the result of careful analysis, though some decisions were made during the construction.

If the general form of the building is dictated by elements in the context, its interior spatiality is a different subject altogether. This is not to say that the interior bears no relation with the context, it does, but the particularities of the context have different implications for the inside of the building. The steep topography prevents a traditional distribution of floors (first, second, third, etc.). Instead, level changes are often irregular, half-level, one-third of a level or, only, 1 metre. Consequently, the challenge inside the building is to connect these continually varying levels while, simultaneously, creating an unambiguous, and functional, circulation system. To achieve this, most circulations are detached from the volumes that contain spaces such as classrooms, offices, toilets, etc. As a result, circulations turn into a network of ramps and bridges that traverse the space at various heights, producing a truly extraordinary spatiality. The effect of such an aerial network of ramps and bridges is exacerbated by the lighting arrangement. Natural sunlight enters generously through the roof, yet this light is broken, as it were, by the ramps which cast a multitude of shadows on the interior walls.

VETERINARY RESEARCH CENTRE, UNIVERSIDAD NACIONAL AUTÓNOMA DE MÉXICO, TEQUISQUIAPAN, MEXICO, ISAAC BROID. GENERAL VIEW OF THE BUILDING FROM THE SOUTH-WEST.

The plasticity of the building is such that it does not need a juxtaposition of materials to create a suitable ambience. Walls are painted white in- and outside the building. White makes the building stand out against the colours of the *cordillera* which change according to the season – or it can make it disappear when it snows. More importantly, white increases the legibility of the curving volumes and alleviates the sense of weight caused by their horizontality. In the interior, free-standing walls have skirting around them while the walls of classrooms and other main spaces have a dado. These two elements serve to highlight the curvature of the walls in the interior, where there is less light. Exterior floors are made of stone, a heavier and resistant material which also works as a transition between the natural and the artificial. The interior floor is presented as a continuous surface throughout. Most ceilings are painted white, although the areas that need extra servicing (reading rooms, auditoria, etc.) use suspended wooden ceilings to conceal the appliances.

These two examples demonstrate the multidimensional character of the work of José Cruz Ovalle. Not only does he carry out adventurous formal explorations, he does so while also attending issues pertaining to the history of the site and the people who use his buildings. Thus, the apparent formalism of his buildings is by no means dissociated from the particularities of context (understood both in its physical and social dimensions). Such a complex simultaneity of factors and design strategies makes Cruz's work an exemplary case of contemporary architectural practice in Latin America.

Veterinary Research Centre, Universidad Nacional Autónoma de México | TEQUISQUIAPAN, MEXICO
Isaac Broid

Isaac Broid, in association with Alfredo Hernández Soto, Lenin García, Miguel Ángel Jiménez, Reynaldo Esperanza, designed a similar educational facility approximately 190 kilometres north-east of Mexico City. The programme for this research complex, Centro de Enseñanza, Investigación y Extensión en Producción Animal en Altiplano, completed in 2007, comprises

VETERINARY RESEARCH CENTRE, UNIVERSIDAD NACIONAL AUTÓNOMA DE MÉXICO. VIEW OF THE AUDITORIUM AND THE LIBRARY BLOCK, RESTING ABOVE THE DORMITORIES.

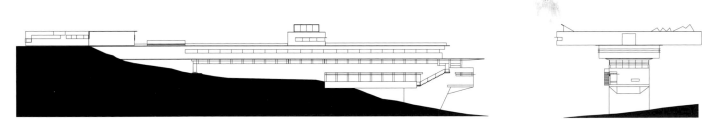

VETERINARY RESEARCH CENTRE, UNIVERSIDAD NACIONAL AUTÓNOMA DE MÉXICO. NORTH AND WEST ELEVATION.

VETERINARY RESEARCH CENTRE, UNIVERSIDAD NACIONAL AUTÓNOMA DE MÉXICO. SOUTH ELEVATION AND CROSS SECTION.

VETERINARY RESEARCH CENTRE, UNIVERSIDAD NACIONAL AUTÓNOMA DE MÉXICO. VIEW OF THE MAIN ACCESS.

VETERINARY RESEARCH CENTRE, UNIVERSIDAD NACIONAL AUTÓNOMA DE MÉXICO. VIEW OF THE AUDITORIUM RESTING OVER THE BLOCK OF DORMITO-RIES AND FRAMING VIEWS OF THE LANDSCAPE.

a wide range of functions: science laboratories, classrooms, study area, administration, library and auditorium as well as accommodation and dining facilities. All these functions had to be condensed in the smallest possible area in order to free space for keeping animals.

Resorting to Donna Haraway,[5] the zoologist, biologist and feminist theorist who has written about mankind's ambivalent relationship with machines and who opposes the simplified categorisation of women, Broid and his team ask: why is the skin the end of the body? This appears to be merely a rhetorical question – the architects do not elaborate further on the theoretical implications of Haraway's work – used suggestively to introduce their intention of designing a building which extends beyond its physical enclosure, its façade (or skin). They

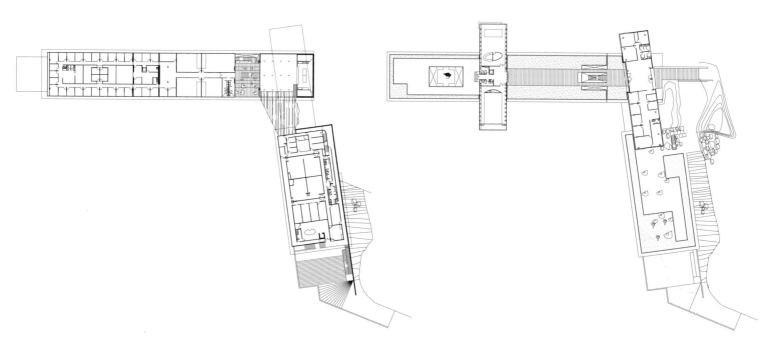

VETERINARY RESEARCH CENTRE, UNIVERSIDAD NACIONAL AUTÓNOMA DE MÉXICO. LOWER LEVEL PLAN (LABORATORIES SOUTH; CUBICLES AND CLASSROOMS NORTH).

VETERINARY RESEARCH CENTRE, UNIVERSIDAD NACIONAL AUTÓNOMA DE MÉXICO. GROUND FLOOR PLAN (ROAD LEVEL, INCLUDING MAIN ACCESS, OFFICES, AUDITORIUM AND LIBRARY).

VETERINARY RESEARCH CENTRE, UNIVERSIDAD NACIONAL AUTÓNOMA DE MÉXICO. ENTRY AREA.

do so by placing the views at the centre of their design agenda. Although responding to the views is the most common way of establishing a link between the building and the context, that is, of exceeding its physicality, Broid refers to this particular building as a viewing platform rather than as a research facility. In fact, he applies this concept to every area of the research centre: the offices, the dormitories, the auditorium, the library, etc., all are considered viewing platforms. At the same time, Broid conceives the centre as a conspicuous element in the landscape, one which encourages the appreciation of the natural surroundings but, at the same time, becomes part of such a view. Hence they have no intention to blend with the natural surroundings but to emerge as an artificial extension of it – an idea which may well derive from their reading of Haraway. The fact that the building is part of the landscape, or context, does not preclude contradiction for Broid. On the contrary, he understands architecture as an irresolute act of negotiation between the natural and the artificial, the building and the user, the architect and the client and so on.

In order to achieve their objectives, the programme was divided in four zones, each of which is housed in a separate volume. The laboratories are situated at the southernmost end of the project in a rectangular volume parallel to the street. Proximity to the street is necessary for reasons of accessibility and maintenance. The laboratories lie 3 metres below the level of the road, that way its roof can be used as a viewing platform adjacent to the road. A second larger block, on the north, contains two levels of dormitories, classrooms, study areas and the cafeteria. The dormitories are placed on the lower floors, at 10.4 and 6.95 metres below street level, forming a plinth which supports the upper floors. The cafeteria, classrooms and study areas are levelled with the laboratories (at -3 metres) so that the roof is also levelled with the road creating a perpendicular platform that extends into the horizon. The administration area is held in an orange rectangular volume which links the previous two zones of the complex. It forms an archway into the field (between the two volumes) and is pierced in the middle to form the main entrance to the complex. The fourth volume, which

LICEO FRANCO-MEXICANO, GUADALAJARA, MEXICO, ALBERTO KALACH. VIEW OF THE CLASSROOMS AND THE ROOF-GARDENS WHICH DOUBLE AS PLAYGROUNDS.

contains the library and the auditorium, sits perpendicularly across the classrooms and study areas in such a way that it cantilevers out on both sides. The administration block and the block containing the library and the auditorium are the only volumes that protrude above street level and interfere with the view from the road. From the bottom of the hill, however, the Veterinary Research Centre does emerge as an imposing ship-like structure which accomplishes the double effect sought by the architect: to magnify the views and to become part of them.

Liceo Franco-Mexicano | GUADALAJARA, MEXICO
Alberto Kalach

Alberto Kalach adopts a similar approach in his design for a school on the north-western suburbs of Guadalajara that was completed in 2005. The area was formerly used for agriculture and farming, but is currently undergoing transformation. In recent years, buildings of various uses have appeared in the

LICEO FRANCO-MEXICANO. THIS IMAGE SHOWS THE RELATIONSHIP BETWEEN THE ADMINISTRATIVE BLOCK (AT THE BACK), THE CLASSROOMS (LEFT) AND THE LEANING PLAYGROUNDS IN FRONT OF EVERY ROW OF CLASSROOMS.

LICEO FRANCO-MEXICANO. VIEW OF THE RETAINING WALL AND THE TOPOGRAPHIC SOLUTION AT THE END OF THE ROW OF CLASSROOMS.

area; these include light industry sheds, educational facilities and residential developments. Some agriculture still persists. As a result the area lacks in character and it is difficult to foresee how it will develop in the future. This initial challenge was complicated by the fact that the programme appeared to be larger than the site. Therefore, it was necessary to devise a strategy in order to minimise land occupation – to provide sufficient space for children to play – while creating an environment that is, simultaneously, friendly but resilient to future changes in the area.

To that end, Kalach and his team located the administrative offices and larger educational units in two blocks along the northern edge of the site. They separate the school from existing buildings and create a grand entrance. In turn, three blocks of classrooms are arranged diagonally in relation to the administration. The rows of classrooms demarcate four distinct sectors. On the west, there is a communal recreational area for all students. Three other areas result between the rows of classrooms; these are used for the recreation of students in the relevant row. The form and disposition of the classrooms is

LICEO FRANCO-MEXICANO. SECTION THROUGH CLASSROOMS AND PLAYGROUNDS.

LICEO FRANCO-MEXICANO. VIEW OF THE INTERIOR OF A CLASSROOM.

LICEO FRANCO-MEXICANO. SITE PLAN.

COLEGIO HONTANARES, EL RETIRO, COLOMBIA, PLAN B ARQUITECTOS. GENERAL VIEW OF THE SCHOOL IN THE LANDSCAPE.

such that they focus on distant views of the mountains, thereby avoiding potential clashes with future constructions nearby. The classrooms are orientated to the south-east in order to receive the morning light, at an angle which facilitates its control by means of vertical elements in the façade. The main feature, however, is the fact that the classrooms are tucked underneath the playground. In other words, the site is treated as a terrain made out of three successive valleys with classrooms underneath.

Unlike previous projects in this chapter, Kalach did not have the privilege to work in a strong and clearly defined landscape. Instead, the school is located in a bland urban periphery not yet consolidated. Consequently, rather than responding to a given landscape, Kalach and his team opted for creating one. Without doubt, the proposed solution generates an interesting spatiality and provides unusual spaces for children to play. It is also an intelligent response to the challenges presented by a tight site. However, it is necessary to wait until the city has grown around the school in order to analyse how such a formidable environment will be affected by surrounding buildings.

Colegio Hontanares | EL RETIRO, COLOMBIA
Plan B Arquitectos

The Colegio Hontanares, whose first phase was completed in 2007, is a medium-scale project in a beautiful and sparsely inhabited mountainous area towards the south-east of Medellín. Unlike the previous project, the Hontanares School sits on a generous site in a decidedly rural location with a steep and irregular topography which, therefore, required a different approach. In order to tackle the complex topography, the architects studied the solutions advanced by the Tayrona culture, an indigenous group that inhabited the Sierra Nevada near the Caribbean coast of Colombia. The Sierra Nevada is an isolated mountain range (it does not belong to the Andes) which rises from an average altitude of 200 metres above sea level at the foothills to approximately 5700 metres at the top (it is the highest mountain in Colombia and the world's highest coastal range). As a result, the *sierra* covers virtually all existing climates and eco-systems, which make it a propitious place to live. On the other hand, the abrupt topography required its inhabitants to develop strategies to adapt the land for both occupation and agriculture. The Tayronas developed a sophisticated system of terraces which followed the contours of the topography in order to facilitate the cultivation and irrigation of crops, as well as the farming of animals. Plan B Arquitectos (Felipe Mesa and Alejandro Bernal) complemented their study of Tayrona land occupation strategies with analyses of Chinese rural architectures which also employ methods of terracing for agricultural purposes. Following their research, Plan B Arquitectos proposed to organise the school on a single narrow linear terrace following the contour lines. This strategy minimises environmental damage and forces the deployment of the project over the entire site, so that it is possible to benefit from a variety of natural conditions and views.

The architects identified four areas on the site: the central plateau, the western hill, the eastern hill and the north-eastern fringe at the bottom of the site. The central plateau is the

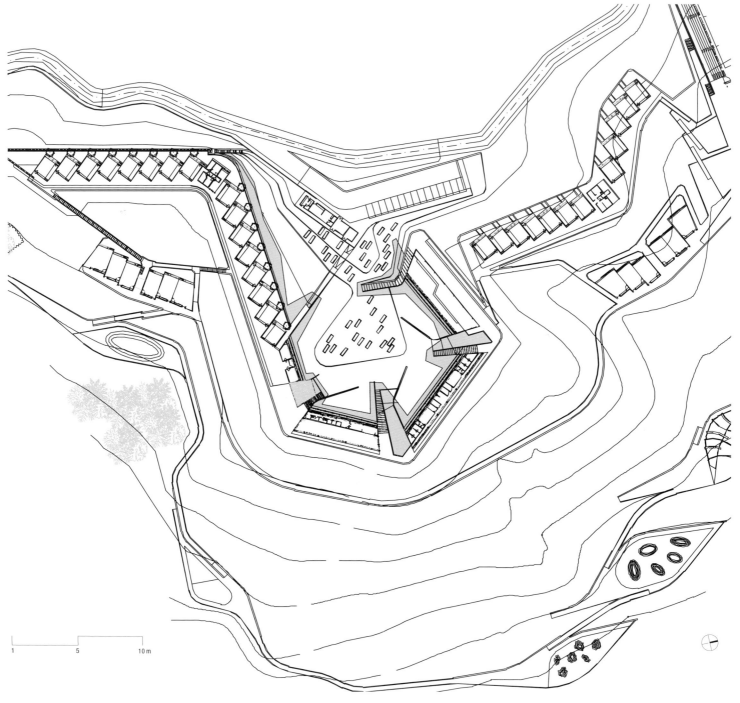

COLEGIO HONTANARES. SITE PLAN.

COLEGIO HONTANARES. VIEW OF THE ROW OF CLASSROOMS.

largest – and only – area of flat land. It is located almost at the centre of the site with views in all directions. For that reason, it was planned as a forecourt and the main public space of the school, the space for weekly assemblies and special events. The non-academic items of the programme (administration,

COLEGIO HONTANARES. INTERIOR OF A COMMUNAL AREA.

teachers' room, etc.) are built around the perimeter of the forecourt but sit 4 metres below it. That way, the building does not interrupt the views and its roof becomes an extension of the upper forecourt into the horizon. The western hill, which is long and gentle, houses the classrooms for the smaller children and the workshops. In turn, the classrooms for students attending the secondary school are located on the eastern hill. This part of the site is narrower, steeper and more secluded, so it is a conducive environment for students who need to concentrate more in order to perform their academic tasks. The remaining part of the site has been articulated by a network of pathways which, like the Tayronas did, generate a succession of terraces at different levels for the cultivation of fruits, an activity students are encouraged to pursue.

The circulation system is simple and unambiguous yet joyful due to the constantly varying views. It consists of a weaving corridor in front of the classrooms which is covered by a concrete canopy. In turn, the canopy doubles as a transitional space between interior and exterior. While the general layout of the building follows the contours of the topography, the rectangular classrooms are orientated in the north-south direc-

COLEGIO HONTANARES. VIEW OF THE UNDULATING ROW OF CLASSROOMS AND THE TERRACING SYSTEM.

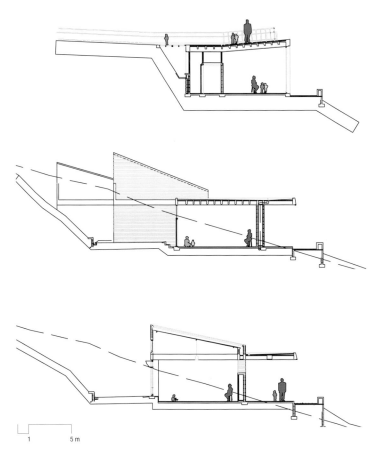

1   5 m

COLEGIO HONTANARES. CROSS SECTIONS THROUGH DIFFERENT AREAS OF THE SCHOOL REVEALING THE INTERESTING INTERPLAY OF SCALES: OFFICES AND PUBLIC AREAS (TOP), MULTI-FUNCTIONAL SPACES (MIDDLE) AND CLASS-ROOMS (BOTTOM).

tion. That way they avoid direct incidence of sunlight, which is carefully controlled by north-facing high windows. The sections reveal an interesting interplay of scales: circulations are relatively shallow, classrooms are high and offices – as well as other non-academic spaces – remain at an intermediate height. The transition between these different scales is emphasised by a series of thresholds which highlight the different spatial charac-teristics of each part of the school. As has been demonstrated throughout this chapter, transitions between interior and exterior, between bright and dark or between hot and cool (or vice versa) are important in dealing with the vast scales and contrasting en-vironmental conditions of the Latin American landscape. In spite of its small scale and formal simplicity, the Hontanares School is a splendid example of the way in which a younger generation of contemporary Colombian architects articulate multiple cultural and architectural elements in order to produce building solu-tions which are both attractive and socially conscious.

Orquideorama | MEDELLÍN, COLOMBIA
Plan B Arquitectos and JPRCR Arquitectos

Orquideorama is a made-up word that describes a garden for the exhibition of orchids. The Orquideorama, built in 2005, belongs to the Jardín Botánico de Medellín, a municipal facility which underwent major renovation during the revitalisation of the northern edge of the city centre. The programme comprises other buildings, amongst which it is worth mentioning the Parque de los Deseos (reviewed earlier) and the Parque Explora (a cultural centre dedicated to the natural sciences). These two facilities and the Botanic Garden are articulated by a station of the city's metro and the partial pedestrianisation of a major intersection.

The architects, Plan B Arquitectos (Felipe Mesa and Alejandro Bernal) and JPRCR Arquitectos (J. Paul Restrepo and Camilo Restrepo), were against the construction of a 'building' which, in their view, would clash with the natural conditions of the garden as well as with the environment where orchids grow. Instead, they conceived a modular system that could develop organically, as a garden, even though the module is artificial. The architects also wanted figuratively to replace the missing foliage of the Botanic Garden in order to complement its existing natural fabric rather than disrupting it. To that end, the proposal consists of a flexible system based on a modular structure that the architects call 'flower-tree'. The name derives from the fact that, in plan, the structure looks like a flower while, in elevation, it looks like a tree. Each module is made of seven hexagons, one in the centre and six more attached to each of its sides. The central hexagon is extruded to become the

ORQUIDEORAMA, MEDELLÍN, COLOMBIA, PLAN B ARQUITECTOS AND JPRCR ARQUITECTOS. GENERAL VIEW OF THE EXHIBITION SPACE UNDER THE 'FLOWER-TREES'

ORQUIDEORAMA. THE TOP OF THE 'FLOWER-TREES' AND THEIR RELATIONSHIP WITH THE CANOPY OF EXISTING TREES.

trunk of the tree-like structure. In fact, much like a tree trunk, the central hexagon provides structural support for the other six – which float above as the canopy of leaves – and contains all the necessary installations (mechanical and electrical). Each 'flower-tree' is an independent structure. Consequently, the project could reduce itself to one single module (if the budget were to run out too early) or could be expanded in the future if it were necessary. Incidentally, the architects proposed 14 'flower-trees' but only 13 were built.

Continuing with their analogy of a tree, the 'petals' of the 'flower-tree' are covered with a translucent material. This creates an environment similar to walking in a forest. The intensity of the light is reduced by the canopy of leaves, but shafts of bright light can penetrate suddenly introducing contrast and excitement. The translucent roof also protects from the rain and collects water that is brought down through the trunk and dropped into the planting beds at the centre of each hexagon. Of course, the fact that orchids grow within the tree trunk and use the nutrients that it brings from the leaves, is part of the architects' straightforward set of biological analogies. Even so, the structures do generate a pleasant open-air exhibition space.

Structurally, the 'flower-tree' consists of a simple tubular metal structure in two parts. In the lower part the six columns are straight and perpendicular to the floor. Approximately 5 metres above the ground the columns meet a horizontal reinforcement and, from that point on, they rotate and lean outwards to meet the vertices of the central hexagon. Since the rotation multiplies the stresses that the structure has to counteract, significant bracing is added in the middle to guarantee its stability and to receive the weight of the trusses which cantilever an average of 10 metres. The metal structure is clad with an intricate wooden lattice which, during the day, filters the sunlight casting interesting shadow patterns on the floor. At night, the structure is magnified by upward lighting which turns the 'flower-trees' into exhibits in their own right.

But if the concept that underpins the project, the audacity of the structure and the impeccable quality of the construction are by all means commendable, it is important to stress that the significance of the Orquideorama as part of the revitalisation of an area of Medellín, lies in the ability of the architects to understand two aspects: on the one hand, the dynamics of change that characterise Colombian cities, on the other, the politics of interaction necessary to conceive this project in relation to others in the area as a way to accomplish the revitalising goal. The former aspect requires that buildings are flexible and adaptable (both in their form and function as well as in their economics). The latter aspect requires architects never to dissociate their buildings from the complex socio-political milieu in which they are embedded. Neither of these two aspects precludes formal experimentation. On the contrary, as the two projects in this part of Medellín that have been studied in this book demonstrate, architects can pursue their own individual agendas while contributing to the consolidation of a collective endeavour. It is also noteworthy that the Orquideorama shows

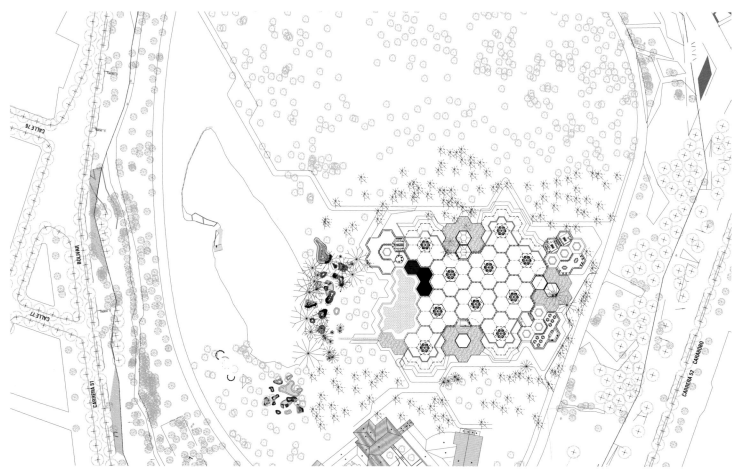

ORQUIDEORAMA. SITE PLAN.

ORQUIDEORAMA. THE METAL STRUCTURE OF THE 'FLOWER-TREES'.

TERMAS GEOMÉTRICAS, PARQUE NACIONAL VOLCÁN VILLARICA, CHILE, GER-MÁN DEL SOL. AERIAL VIEW OF THE QUINCHO IN THE CANYON WITH ZIGZAG-GING WALKWAYS AND ARTIFICIAL BATHING PONDS.

TERMAS GEOMÉTRICAS. VIEW OF ONE OF THE BATHING PONDS AND THE SCAT-TERED RED GRASS-ROOFED WOODEN STRUCTURES.

the extraordinary versatility of a young group of architects who embrace each project as a different challenge and deliberately refuse to be located within particular architectural movements.

Termas Geométricas |

Parque Nacional Volcán Villarica, Chile
Germán del Sol

To conclude this chapter on different architectural responses to Latin American landscapes, I will examine a project designed by Germán del Sol in the south of Chile. The merit of this project, completed in 2005, lies not only in its formal exuber-ance but, also, in the subtle interpretation of the practice of outdoor bathing. Going on a trip with family or friends to bathe in rivers is a common and well-liked activity amongst Chilean people – as it is in many other Latin American countries. The trip involves a certain ceremony. It all begins with getting there,

TERMAS GEOMÉTRICAS. VIEW OF THE SUCCESSION OF BATHING PONDS AND CHANGING FACILITIES WITH THE HOT SPRINGS SPURTING OUT OF THE VOL-CANIC ROCKS.

TERMAS GEOMÉTRICAS. VIEW OF THE ZIGZAGGING WALKWAYS ALONG THE CANYON.

for usually bathing areas are remote and require travelling. Once the river has been reached, the party walks along the river bank to find the perfect spot. It has to be wide enough to set up a temporary camp, often suitable for cooking (but not always) and, also, it needs a nice deep pond for swimming. Preferably, the site ought to be private. In fact, there are, even, certain rules

of etiquette according to which people avoid sites that have already been taken by others. In sum, river bathing is associated with the concepts of journey, search and setting camp while being governed by a complex tacit social politics.

Let me now describe briefly the region where the project is located as a means to reiterate the relevance of the previous argument. The Parque Nacional Volcán Villarica is located in the south of Chile, approximately 600 kilometres south of Santiago. It shares the name with a lake and the nearest town, which sits on the lake's shore. The Villarica is an active volcano – indeed, it is one of the most active volcanoes in the country – and is permanently covered in snow. The surrounding landscape is marked by the traces of previous eruptions, by numerous fresh water rivers and by hundreds of volcanic hot springs all embedded in a rugged topography and dense vegetation.

The project can be described quite simply. It consists of a 450-metre-long elevated walkway – or bridge – which hovers over the river, zigzagging along the narrow canyon. The walkway connects 20 man-made ponds that were carved in the rock on both sides of the canyon and distributed in such a way that they are separate from each other, remaining somewhat private. The ponds mix the water that spurts out of the rock at 80°C and combines it with fresh water from the river to achieve a pleasant temperature. Some ponds are large and shallow, for families with children, for example, others are deep for accomplished swimmers. There are also smaller ponds for private bathing – or a little more intimacy. Each pond has a terrace where bathers can keep their belongings, pick-nick or cook. Changing facilities and toilets are scattered through the length of the project, more or less equidistantly from the ponds. At the end of the walkway there is a *quincho*, a small wooden shed, with an open fire where food is served and people can gather to talk. It is a transitional space, the end of the journey by road and the beginning of the journey into the mountain on foot, as well as vice versa.

Del Sol uses distinctly geometric forms, linear but angular, in order to produce a separation between the natural and the man-made. That is why the walkway and other structures are

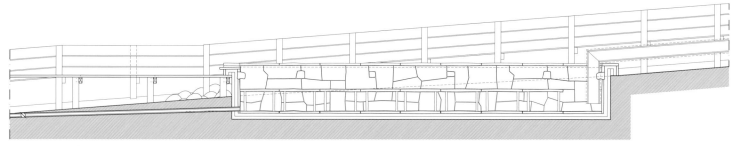

TERMAS GEOMÉTRICAS. SECTION THROUGH ONE OF THE BATHING PONDS WITH WALKWAY AND ACCESS.

TERMAS GEOMÉTRICAS. VIEW OF THE CANDLELIT FLOOR LEVEL 'LAMPS' ALONG THE WALKWAYS WITH CHANGING ROOM IN THE BACKGROUND (AND BATHING POND ON THE RIGHT).

TERMAS GEOMÉTRICAS. VIEW OF THE RED ZIGZAGGING WALKWAYS STANDING OUT IN THE STEAM FROM THE HOT VOLCANIC WATER.

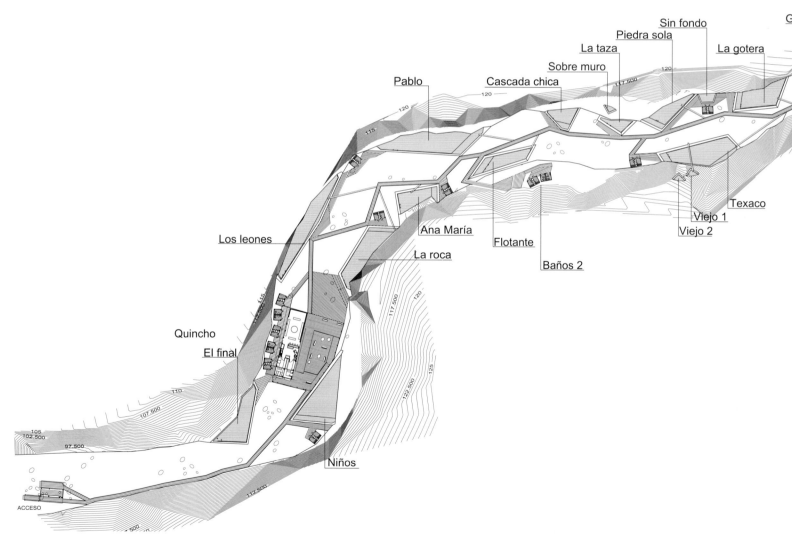

TERMAS GEOMÉTRICAS. SITE PLAN.

elevated from the ground: to formalise such distinction and to disrupt nature the least possible. The ponds, which are inevitably embedded into the mountain, juxtapose linear concrete dikes clad in local slate with the natural rock. This accentuates the distinction between the two aspects of the project: natural and artificial. That is also the case with the red dye applied to the coigüe local wood. Red enhances visibility when dark falls or when the steam rises up from the water, but it also sets the project apart from the dominant green and grey colours of the site. But if del Sol was at odds to establish a relationship of separation, the vegetated roofs introduce a contradictory desire

to blend with the landscape. Indeed, such a contradiction sums up the fundamental nature of the project, it lies at the border between architecture and landscape or, even, between architecture and popular building (vernacular architecture). Furthermore, the project departs from the typology of the traditional Chilean *terma* in order to explore alternative formal possibilities.[6] However, it remains connected with the tradition of outdoor bathing and the tacit politics that determine its performance. In other words, this excellent example of architecture and landscape architecture is not without inherent contradictions. Nonetheless, those contradictions are the reason why the project is unique.

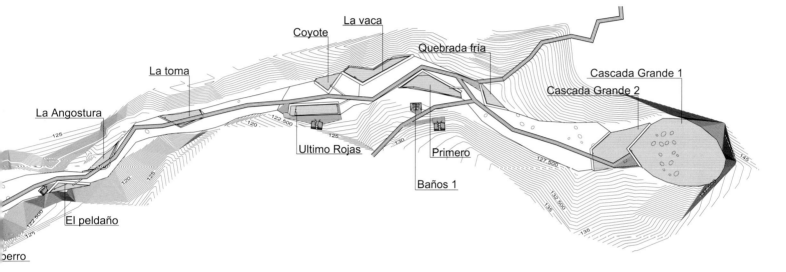

1   In fact these two volcanoes belong to a volcanic chain of six strato-volcanoes along 25 kilometres of border between the two countries.
2   The Chilean pavilion at the Seville World Exposition was designed by José Cruz Ovalle in association with Germán del Sol.
3   José Cruz Ovalle explains his design methodology and his take on the notion of abstraction in the

book *Hacia una Nueva Abstracción* (Towards a New Abstraction), a monograph dedicated to his work edited by Alejandro Crispiani and Elizabeth Bennett. Santiago: Escuela de Arquitectura de la Pontificia Universidad Católica de Chile, 2004.
4   Indeed, Cruz received the Finnish Spirit of Nature Wood Architecture Award for the extensive and extraordinary use of this material in his work.

5   See Haraway, D., *Simians, Cyborgs and Women: The Reinvention of Nature.* London/New York: Routledge, 1991.
6   The *terma* is the expression used to describe places for bathing in thermal water that spurts out of the rocks in the volcanic Andean regions of Chile. Culturally, however, the *terma* refers to the tradition of bathing and the activities associated with it.

SELECTED BIBLIOGRAPHY

Anderson, B., *Imagined Communities: Reflections on the Origin and Spread of Nationalism*. London/New York: Verso, (1983) 2006.

Andreoli, E. and A. Forty (eds.), *Brazil's Modern Architecture*. London: Phaidon, 2004.

Arango, S. (ed.), *Historia de la Arquitectura en Colombia*. Bogotá: Centro Editorial y Facultad de Artes Universidad Nacional de Colombia, 1993.

Arango, S., *Modernidad y Postmodernidad en América Latina: Estado del Debate*. Bogotá: Escala, 1991.

Beverley, J., *Subalternity and Representation: Arguments in Cultural Theory*. Durham: Duke University Press, 1999.

Beverley, J. et al. (eds.), *The Postmodernism Debate in Latin America*. Durham: Duke University Press, 1993.

Bhabha, H. K., *The Location of Culture*. London: Routledge, 1994.

Borden, I. and J. Rendell (eds.), *Intersections: Architectural Histories and Critical Theories*. London: Routledge, 2000.

Brillembourg, C. (ed.), *Latin American Architecture 1929–1960: Contemporary Reflections*. New York: Princeton Architectural Press, 2004.

Browne, E., *Otra Arquitectura en América Latina*. Naucalpan: Gustavo Gili de México, 1988.

Castro, R., *Rogelio Salmona*. Bogotá: Villegas Editores, 1998.

Castro, R., *Rogelio Salmona: A Tribute*. Bogotá: Villegas Editores, 2009.

Crispiani, A. and E. Bennett (eds.), *Hacia una Nueva Abstracción*. Santiago: Escuela de Arquitectura de la Pontificia Universidad Católica de Chile, 2004.

Curtis, W. J. R., *Modern Architecture since 1900*. London: Phaidon, (1982) 2000.

De Grangis, R. and Z. Bernd, *Unforseeable Americas: Questioning Cultural Hybridity in the Americas*. Amsterdam/New York: Rodopi, 2000.

Evenson, N., *Two Brazilian Capitals: Architecture and Urbanism in Rio de Janeiro and Brasilia*. New Haven: Yale University Press, 1973.

Fernández Cox, C., 'Modernidad Apropiada', in Arango, S. (ed.), *Modernidad y Postmodernidad en América Latina: Estado del Debate*. Bogotá: Escala, 1991.

Fraser, V., *Building the New World: Studies in the Modern Architecture of Latin America 1930–1960*. London: Verso, 2000.

García Canclini, N., *Las Culturas Populares del Capitalismo*. Mexico City: Editorial Nueva Imagen, 1982.

García Canclini, N., *Consumidores y Ciudadanos: Conflictos Multiculturales de la Globalización*. Mexico City: Editorial Grijalbo, 1995.

García Canclini, N., *Culturas Híbridas: Estrategias para Entrars y Salir de la Modernidad*. Mexico City: Editorial Paidós, 2002 (reprint). – English edition: *Hybrid Cultures: Strategies for Entering and Leaving Modernity*. Minneapolis: University of Minnesota Press, 1995.

Haraway, D., *Simians, Cyborgs and Women: The Reinvention of Nature*. London/New York: Routledge, 1991.

Hernández, F., P. Kellet and L. Allen, *Rethinking the Informal City: Critical Perspectives from Latin America*. Oxford/New York: Berghahn Books, 2009.

Hernández, F., M. Millington and I. Borden, *Transculturation: Cities, Spaces and Architectures in Latin America*. Amsterdam/New York: Rodopi, 2005.

Holston, J., *The Modernist City: An Anthropological Critique of Brasilia*, Chicago/London: University of Chicago Press, 1989.

Larsen, N., *Reading North by South: On Latin American Literature, Culture, and Politics*. Minneapolis: University of Minnesota Press, 1995.

Lejeune, J. F. (ed.), *Cruelty and Utopia: Cities and Landscapes of Latin America*. New York: Princeton Architectural Press, 2005.

Liernur, J. F., *Arquitectura en la Argentina de Siglo XX*. Buenos Aires: Fondo Nacional de Artes, 2001.

Ortiz, F., *Cuban Counterpoint: Tobacco and Sugar*. Durham: Duke University Press, 1995.

Pratt, M. L., *Imperial Eyes: Travel Writing and Transculturation*. London: Routledge, 1992.

Quantrill, M. *Latin American Architecture: Six Voices*. Austin: Texas A&M University Press, 2000.

Rakesh, M., *Understanding the Developing Metropolis: Lessons from the City Study of Bogotá and Cali, Colombia*. Oxford: Oxford University Press, 1994.

Rama, A., *The Lettered City*. Durham: Duke University Press, 1996.

Rama, A., 'Processes of Transculturation in Latin American Narrative', in *The Journal of Latin American Cultural Studies*, Vol. 6, No. 2, 1997.

Saldarriaga, A., *Arquitectura para Todos los Días: La Práctica Cultural de la Arquitectura*. Bogotá: Centro Editorial Universidad Nacional de Colombia, 1988.

Segre, R., F. Kusnetzoff and E. Grossman (eds.), *Latin America in Its Architecture*. Teaneck, New Jersey: Holmes & Meier Publishers, 1982.

Téllez, G., *Rogelio Salmona: Arquitectura y Poética del Lugar*. Bogotá: Escala, 1991.

Turner, J. F. C., *Housing by People: Towards Autonomy in Building Environments*. London: Marion Boyars, 1976.

UNESCO, *World Heritage List*. Paris/New York: UNESCO, No. 445, 1987.

Villanueva, P., *Carlos Raúl Villanueva*. Sevilla: Tanais, 2000. – English edition: *Carlos Raúl Villanueva*, Basel: Birkhäuser, 2000.

Weber, J. and J. Rausch, *Where Cultures Meet: Frontiers in Latin American History*. Wilmington, Delaware: Scholarly Resources Inc., 1994.

Werbner, P. and T. Modood, *Debating Cultural Hybridity: Multi-Cultural Identities and the Politics of Anti-Racism* (Postcolonial Encounters Series). London: ZED Books, 1997.

Yudice, G., J. Franco and J. Florez J. (eds.), *On Edge: The Crisis of Contemporary Latin American Culture*. Minneapolis: University of Minnesota Press, 1992.

ABOUT THE AUTHOR

Felipe Hernández was born in Colombia and is an architect and professor of architectural design, history and theory at the University of Cambridge. He has an MA in architecture and critical theory and received his PhD from the University of Nottingham. He taught previously in the School of Architecture at the University of Liverpool, and has also lectured at the Bartlett School of Architecture (UCL), the Universities of Nottingham and East London in the United Kingdom as well as Brown University in the USA and the Bauhaus Dessau Foundation in Germany. Felipe Hernández has written extensively on contemporary architectures in Latin America, formulating a revision of the way in which such architectures are theorised and inscribed in the history of the field. His most recent publication, *Bhabha for Architects* (Routledge, 2009), explores the contribution of the postcolonial critic Homi K. Bhabha to architecture, both its theory and professional practice. Additionally, Felipe Hernández is co-editor of *Rethinking the Informal City: Critical Perspectives from Latin America* (Berghahn Books, 2009) and *Transculturation: Cities, Spaces and Architectures in Latin America* (Rodopi, 2005).

ACKNOWLEDGEMENTS

First, I would like to thank Ria Stein, from Birkhäuser, for her interest in the project and her support since the beginning. Ria offered invaluable and useful advice which made the realisation of the book possible.

I must also thank the Royal Institute of British Architects which awarded me the Modern Architecture and Town Planning Trust Award in 2007. This award was decisive in permitting the practical realisation of the project. Similarly, the School of Architecture at the University of Liverpool offered their support by financing part of the travel costs around Latin America to visit many of the buildings studied and illustrated in the book.

I am also greatly indebted to all the architects whose work is included in this publication for their kind and timely collaboration. Without exception, architects were quick to submit their images of their projects, as well as explicative material. Many of them welcomed me to their offices, some to their homes, took me to their buildings and dedicated time to talk about themselves, their practices and their work. I spent several hours on the telephone – or the internet – talking to those I was unable to visit personally due to reasons of time and distance. My gratitude goes also to colleagues at the University of Liverpool, David Dunster and Neil Jackson, for their advice on historical and theoretical matters. They convinced me that not every aspect could be tackled and that, inevitably, many topics would be left out, topics which would need to be explained elsewhere and in the future. Thanks also to Carolina Rodriguez who read the introduction when my eyes could no longer see all the words that I had written; she offered insightful comments. Other architects, theorists and historians contributed to to the making of this book in many ways: Guillermina Abeledo, Benjamin Barney, Keith Eggerner, Andres Felipe Erazo, Jorge Francisco Liernur and Claudia Schmidt. Similarly, I must thank the photographers who kindly contributed their wonderful images and, so, facilitated the materialisation of this publication. Others participated indirectly in this project and, in this vein, I must thank Mark Millington, Jane Rendell, Iain Borden and Ricardo Castro for conversations, methodological guidance and, above all, for their support during the past ten years of academic work. I apologise to those whose names I may have forgotten here, but who also helped me to take this project to completion.

Finally, I would like to thank my wife Lea for listening to my endless monologues about Latin American architecture, for questioning my methods and theories and, more importantly, for being so patient when I was away either travelling or writing. I am immensely grateful for her support.

INDEX

ILLUSTRATION CREDITS

1 INTRODUCTION
7, 8, 9 ANDRÉS GOÑI; 10 MARIA AMELIA
SANCHEZ CASELLA; 11, 12 ANNALISA SPENCER;
13 PAULO AFONSO RHEINGANTZ; 14, 15T GUSTAVO
JIMÉNEZ; 15B, 16–17 P. VILLANUEVA, *CARLOS
RAÚL VILLANUEVA*, BASEL: BIRKHÄUSER, 2000;
20, 21 RICARDO L. CASTRO; 22 KEITH EGGENER

2 BUILDING ON THE CITY'S EDGE
24 SERGIO GOMEZ; 25, 26T, 27T NELSON KON;
28, 29T, 30L, 31, 32T SERGIO GOMEZ AND JUAN
PABLO BUITRAGO; 33B, 34T, 35, 36B SERGIO
GOMEZ AND LORENZO CASTRO; 38, 39, 40, 41
URBAN THINK TANK

3 PUBLIC SPACES AS CONTACT ZONES
42 LORENZO CASTRO; 43, 44T, 45 PABLO CORRAL;
46, 47, 48, 49, 50 LORENZO CASTRO; 51, 52T
G. OLAVE AND G. ABELEDO; 53, 54, 55T, 56L
ALESSANDRO DESOGOS, SERGIO ESMORIS, SERGIO
SABAG, LUIS ETCHEGORRY, CLAUDIO VEKSTEIN

4 DESIGNING FOR POVERTY
58 EDUARDO HIROSE; 59, 60, 61, 62T, 63T, 64B,
65T, 66T, 67 ELEMENTAL; 68T, 69T, 70, 71T ANA
ELVIRA VÉLEZ; 73B, 74, 75 EDUARDO HIROSE AND
ALEXIA LEÓN

5 THE PRIVATE HOUSE
76 SERGIO GOMEZ; 77, 78, 79 SYLVIA PATIÑO;
81 AND COVER PHOTOGRAPH, 82, 83T NELSON
KON; 84, 85T, 86 GABINETE DE ARQUITECTURA;
87, 88T ISAAC BROID; 89, 90T, 91, 93T, 93B
MATHIAS KLOTZ ARQUITECTO; 94T, 95T NICOLÁS
CAMPODONICO; 96T, 97T, 98T, 98B GUSTAVO
FRITTEGOTTO; 99T, 99B, 100T IWAN BAAN,
TATIANA BILBAO, CARLOS LEGUIZAMO, COURTESY
OF KURIMANZUTTO; 101, 102T NICOLÁS
CAMPODONICO; 103, 104T, 105, 106, 107 SERGIO
GOMEZ; 108 (ALL PHOTOS), 109 IWAN BAAN; 110,
111, 112 PAÚL RIVERA/ARCHPHOTO.COM

6 ARCHITECTURE IN THE LANDSCAPE
114 FELIPE HERNÁNDEZ; 115, 116T, 117T, 118,
119T, 120T, 120C, 121 GUY WEMBORNE AND GUY
ST. CLAIR; 122R, 123T JUAN PURCELL AND
SEBASTIÁN SEPÚLVEDA; 125, 126T, 127 JUAN
PURCELL AND ROLAND HALBE; 128, 129T, 130T,
131 ISAAC BROID; 132, 133T, 134 ALBERTO
KALACH ARQUITECTOS; 135, 137, 138T PLAN B
ARQUITECTOS; 139, 141 PLAN B ARQUITECTOS/
JPRCR ARQUITECTOS; 142, 143T, 144T GUY
WEMBORNE, GUY ST. CLAIR AND GERMÁN DEL SOL

T: TOP
B: BOTTOM
L: LEFT
R: RIGHT
C: CENTRE

UNLESS NOTED OTHERWISE, ALL PLANS AND
DRAWINGS WERE PROVIDED BY THE ARCHITEC-
TURAL PRACTICES.

WE ARE ESPECIALLY GRATEFUL TO THESE IMAGE
PROVIDERS. EVERY REASONABLE ATTEMPT HAS
BEEN MADE TO IDENTIFY OWNERS OF COPYRIGHT.
SHOULD UNINTENTIONAL MISTAKES OR OMIS-
SIONS HAVE OCCURRED, WE SINCERELY APOLO-
GISE AND ASK FOR NOTICE. SUCH MISTAKES WILL
BE CORRECTED IN THE NEXT EDITION OF THIS
PUBLICATION.